HEROICA

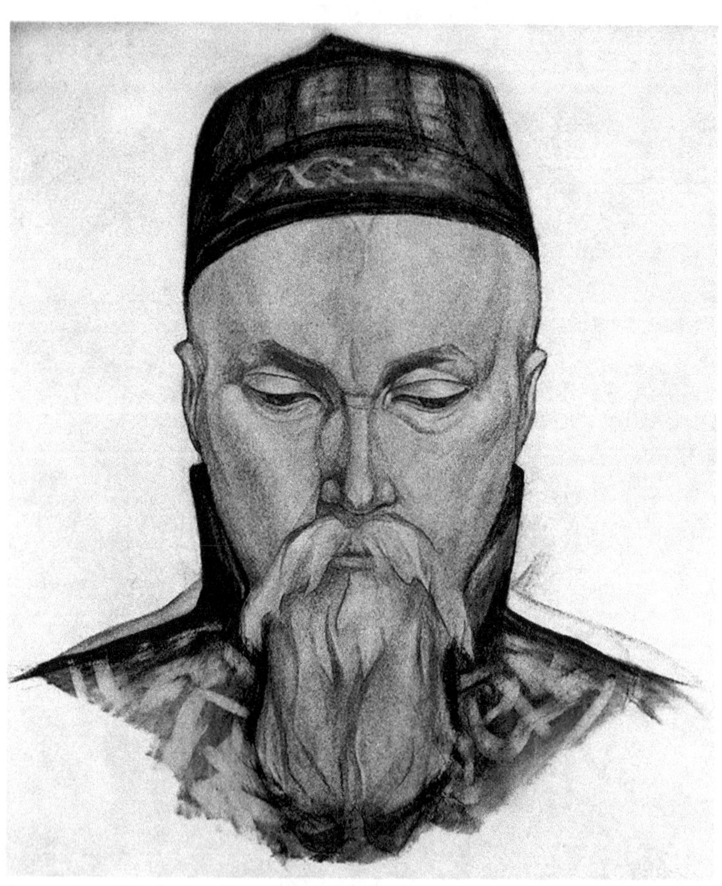

Portrait of Nicholas Roerich by Svetoslav Roerich

HEROICA

NICHOLAS ROERICH

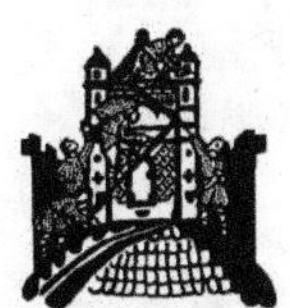

NICHOLAS ROERICH MUSEUM

NEW YORK   MMXVIII

Nicholas Roerich Museum
319 West 107th Street
New York NY 10025
www.roerich.org

Cover illustration:
Nicholas Roerich. *Great Spirit of the Himalayas.* 1934.

PUBLISHER'S NOTE

THE fate of this book is unusual, and the book has followed a somewhat long and winding path to publication. After Nicholas Roerich compiled *Heroica* in 1946, he sent it off to an Indian publishing house. But the economic difficulties following the Second World War, coupled with Roerich's passing in 1947, halted its immediate publication. After many decades, the manuscript was discovered in our archive, and we are pleased and honored to be able to publish it at long last. Readers and followers of Roerich's prodigious output of written texts can now enjoy a new book in the series, *Nicholas Roerich: Collected Writings.*

You may wonder if it is still relevant after all these years. Roerich wrote the essays in this book during the 1930s and 40s, an era that now seems far removed from our own. Yet his perspective focuses on the universal and his messages resonate today just as powerfully as they did when he first wrote them. His most fundamental message, one that weaves its way throughout all of his work, both on the page and on the canvas, is this: that culture—its celebration and preservation—is the basis for creating a better future for all mankind.

Without exaggeration, the treasures of culture are the stronghold of a nation. The entire upbuilding—all enlightenment, all spiritual inspiration, all happiness and salvation—will be born upon the foundation of cultural treasures.

Nicholas Roerich

Among the many ideas Roerich discusses in this book are: the power of beauty and wisdom, the importance of respecting all living beings, and the need for creating art with limitless potential. Roerich remains ever hopeful, which speaks to the strength of his convictions despite the uncertainty and conflict of this time. Here, he proves himself to be a thought leader in the philosophy of culture and its place in our society.

As his work continues to resonate with people from all over the world, we hope that this book will find its way on to the shelves and libraries of readers who care about art, culture and their fate in future generations.

We would like to thank all those who helped in the preparation of this book, and without whom its publication would not have been possible. Our special thanks go to White Mountain Education Association, particularly to Joleen Dianne DuBois and Kathryn Agrell, who worked so assiduously on editing the texts.

CONTENTS

IV. ON TO THE SUMMITS

V. GREEN LEAVES

VI. LET US HOPE

I
SONGS CELESTIAL

FEARS

"THE sun set. Forest murmurs began. The crowns of old oaks appeared as monstrous silhouettes. The gigantic pines turned red. Flowers glimmered like horrible eyes. The ravines became pitch black and the boulders protruded like huge skulls. Look, what a terrible face the forest shows!

"The crane hurried into the meadow and gabbled: "Beware, beware!" and disappeared behind the trees.

And above, in the foliage, the raven croaked: "*Finis! Finis!*"

The thrush above screamed: "Terrible! Terrible!"

The oriole whistled: "Oh, you poor fellow!"

From the top of the tree appeared a starling that took pity: "A good lad is lost. Pity. Pity."

And the woodpecker persisted: "Let him, let him!"

The magpie gossiped as if in the bazaar: "Let us rush to tell them. Let us rush to tell them!"

And even the peaceful bullfinch squeaked: "It is bad, very bad!"

"How many fears! From the earth, from the trees, from the sky—whistling, crackling, and hissing. It seemed as if all the snakes rose from the grass—no help, no escape! And on the path there was standing the bear himself. What else, if not a bear, could that black spot be? And these flashing lights are not fireflies but also something horrible.

"Under the enchanted rock, an unknown wizard had settled. And he caught birds with ingenious traps. And he taught every bird one word. And the wanderers became frightened and pale, hearing this horrible judgment of the birds. And the wizard smiled; he listened to the birds and they brought no fear to him. Only he was aware that they knew no more and could say nothing else."

Are not all horrible words like this gabbling of birds? And is not the terrible bear but a rotten tree stem? And are not the ghostly snakes but twigs in the grass? And who are these mysterious wizards who teach the gospel of fear? Who was the primogenious being who, in a language unknown to us, for the first time uttered the cursed word "fear"? And was this first fright a real horror, or was it a ghastly mirage? But millenniums and cruel atavism embodied this first cry of horror into generations. The inexperienced youth and grey wiseacres in sinister unison began to sing the hymn of fear. There was created an entire cult of horror. But what has a striving, honest man to fear?

All the lightning and thunder of the Universe teach us that there is nothing to fear—one has but to know. The wise heart convinces the brain that fear is the most absurd invention. The highest ordainments proclaim that the human spirit is eternal and cannot be harmed. People read this Truth, and yet the habit of atavism, of fear rips them and crushes them to the earth. They do not listen to the voice of the heart. Science itself comes to aid the heart. All the latest strivings of science prove that knowledge frees man from fear. How many wonderful basic energies are unveiled by science! And human life can be absolutely transmuted.

But *terror antiquus*—the ancient terror still reigns. People still fear to know. For the majority of people, science is still sorcery. *Horribile dictu*, but humanity is not far from medieval superstitions, when for every desire to know, people were burned at the stake or beheaded. It makes no difference that the inquisition of today applies, instead of fire, still more cruel methods. Fire destroyed the body, but many other methods torture the spirit; and in their evil inventiveness, they subject the world to convulsions of horror. Under various pretexts, by various forms of scarecrows, someone tries to prohibit and deny. We all know these deniers. And what is at the bottom of this crass ignorance? Open the crude-colored feathers of the bloated ignoramus and you will discover the grey feather of fear—and as the hair stands on end, so does this feather rise, not from noble indignation but from ugly fear alone.

Every cognizance is already fearless. And liberated science is also fearless. Everyone ascending the summit, at the moment of having made this decision, already rejects fear. There is deep significance in the advice that one should apply medicinal help against fear. So much is said about suggestion. Research of psychic energy becomes a science, and should not all sciences be turned first of all toward the annihilation of fear?

Fear is an attribute of ignorance. Fear is poison. Fear is fossilization. Fear is paralysis. Fear is defeat. Fear is decay. Fear is destruction. Fear is annihilation.

In *The Ring of the Nibelung*, the sorcerer Mime tests Siegfried because a hero is needed who does not know fear. Mime tries to frighten young Siegfried with abominable horrors, but the hero simply does not know what fear means. Mime describes to him the terrible dragon, but Siegfried only asks where he can find the monster. The spirit of the hero does not know the shackles of fear.

Every hero, when seeking attainment, is free from fear. All ordainments preach fearlessness as the motive power of evolution.

From the East resounded the great ordainment: "*Mā bhāyi*"—"Fear not!"

In response to this mighty command, there thundered from the depths of ages: "Warriors, warriors, we call ourselves. We fight for noble virtue, for lofty effort, for sublime wisdom. For this reason we call ourselves warriors!"

GLORY TO WOMEN, BEARERS OF CULTURE

FROM heart to heart!

Culture is reverence of Light. Culture is love of humanity. Culture is fragrance, the unity of life and beauty. Culture is the synthesis of uplifting and sensitive attainments. Culture is the armor of Light. Culture is salvation. Culture is the motivating power. Culture is the Heart.

If we gather all the definitions of Culture, we find the synthesis of active Bliss, the altar of enlightenment and constructive beauty.

Condemnation, disparagement, defying, melancholy, disintegration, and all other characteristics of ignorance do not befit culture. The great tree of Culture is nourished by an unlimited knowledge, by enlightened labor, incessant creativeness, and noble attainment.

The cornerstones of great civilizations support the stronghold of Culture. But from the tower of Culture, there radiates the jewel—adamant from the loving, realizing, and dauntless Heart.

Love opens these beautiful Gates. As with each true key, so also must this love be true, and Culture self-sacrificing, daring, fiery. Where we find the sources of Culture, they are fiery and issue from the very depths. Where culture has once been born, it cannot be killed. One may annihilate civilization, but Culture, the true spiritual treasure, is eternal.

Therefore, the field of Culture is a joyful one, joyful even during labor, joyful even during the tense battles with the most obscure ignorance. The flaming heart is without limitations in the great Infinity.

The Festival of Labor and Constructiveness! A summons to this Festival means a reminder of eternal labor, of the joy of responsibility and of human dignity.

The labor of the worker for Culture is like the work of a physician. The true physician is acquainted with more than one disease. And not only does the physician cure that which has already occurred, but his wise foresight anticipates the future. The physician not only eradicates the illness, but he labors to improve the health for the whole of life. The physician descends into the darkest cellars in order to carry light and warmth there.

The physician is not forgetful of all the amelioration and beautification of life, in order to give joy to the understanding spirit. The physician not only knows of the old epidemics, but he readily acquaints himself with the symptoms of new diseases, which have been induced by the decay of the foundations.

The physician has sage words of counsel for the young and for the old, and is ready to give everyone encouraging advice. The physician does not cease to extend his knowledge, otherwise he could not answer the needs of the present. The physician does not lose patience or tolerance because a restraint of feeling would repel the suffering ones from him.

The physician does not fear the sight of human ulcers because he is concerned only with their cure. The physician collects various curative herbs and stones; he knows the research for their benevolent application. The physician is not weary of hastening with and for the suffering ones at all hours of the day or night.

All these qualities are also inherent in the worker for Culture. He is equally ready at all hours of the day or night to contribute his help. The worker for Culture always beneficently answers: "I am always ready!" His heart is ever open to everything in which experience and knowledge may be useful. Helping, he himself continually learns, because "in giving, we receive." He is not afraid, for he knows that fear opens the gates of darkness.

The worker for Culture is always youthful, for his heart does not wither. He is movable because movement is force. He stands vigil on the parapet of Bliss, Knowledge, and Beauty. He knows what true cooperation is.

All coworkers for Culture are united by rays of the heart. Mountains and oceans are no obstacles to these flaming hearts. They are not dreamers but constructors and smiling plowmen.

In sending this Greeting of Culture, one cannot do so without a smile, without the call of friendship. Thus we shall meet, thus we shall gather together and labor for Bliss, Beauty, and Knowledge. And we shall do this undeferrably, without losing a day, nor an hour, in blissful constructiveness.

Mothers, wives, and sisters—transform the dusky daily life into the festival of Great Service, and show the coming generation that every labor, while of spiritual aspect, creates high quality. This sublime quality should enter human life from dawn to sunset, and in this constant self-perfectment, we will find the creative smile of happiness.

Mothers, wives, and sisters—create heroes!

May the blessings of the Mother of the World be with you!

CHANDOGYA UPANISHADS

"THE breath is saturated; the eye is saturated; the sun is saturated; the heavens are saturated. Everything under the sky and under the sun is saturated.

"Whence then is all that takes place saturated: herds, nourishment, strength, splendor, solemnity of Service?"

"Viyana is saturated; the earth is saturated; the moon is saturated; the heavenly dominions are saturated. Everything beneath them and beneath the moon is saturated.

"Whence then is all that takes place saturated: herds, nourishment, strength, splendor, solemnity of service?"

"Anana is saturated; the world is saturated; fire is saturated; earth is saturated. Everything under fire and earth is saturated.

"Whence then is all that takes place saturated: herds, nourishment, strength, splendor, solemnity of Service?"

"Samana is saturated; spirit is saturated; vortices are saturated; the hurricane is saturated. Everything beneath the vortices in the hurricane is saturated.

"Whence then is all that takes place saturated: herds, nourishment, strength, splendor, solemnity of Service?"

"Udana is saturated; air is saturated; space is saturated. Everything aerial and spatial is saturated.

"Whence then is all that takes place saturated: herds, nourishment, strength, splendor, solemnity of Service?"

"Whoever, knowing this, serves Agnihotra, serves in all worlds, in all that exists, in everything."

"As children huddle together around the mother, so do beings cluster around Agnihotra—around Agnihotra."

* * *

"All has been spiritualized from the Subtlest Entity. This is the sole Reality. This is Atman."

"Verily, dead is the body, abandoned by the spirit. The spirit then does not die. All has been spiritualized by the Subtlest Entity. This is the sole Reality, this is Atman."

"Cast this salt in the water and return to me tomorrow morning."

"Taste now this water, what do you find?" "It is salty." "Draw from this water more deeply, what do you find?" "It is salty." "Taste it from the bottom. What do you find?" "It is salty." "Taste again and come here to me." "It is all the same." "Thus, verily, my friend, you still do not notice the essence, yet it is everywhere."

* * *

"Tell me all that you know, and I will tell you what follows."

"I know the Rig-Veda, the Yajur-Veda, the Sama-Veda, the Atharva-Veda, the ancient sayings, the Veda of Vedas; I know the ceremonials; I know calculations, the science of predictions, weather forecasting, logic, the rules of behavior, etymology, the science of sacred texts, the science of arms, astronomy, the facts about the serpent and the djinn. That is what I know."

"All that you have enumerated are only words."

"Words—Rig-Veda and Yajur-Veda, and Sama-Veda, and Atharva-Veda and ancient sayings, and the science of predictions, and the perception of time, and logic, and the rules of behavior, and etymology, and the science of sacred texts, and the science of arms, and astronomy, and the science of the serpent and the djinn; all these are only words. Apprehend the proper understanding of words."

"When one understands in the words of Brahman, he can do all that he wishes within the power of these words."—"Teacher, tell this to me."

"It, the Word, is verily greater than all words. This

Word enables one to understand the Rig-Veda, and the Yajur-Veda, and the Sama-Veda, and the Atharva-Veda and the ancient sayings, and grammar, and the rules of calculation, and the science of predictions, and knowledge of time, and logic, and the rules of behavior, and etymology, and the science of sacred texts, and the science of arms, and astronomy, and the knowledge of the serpents and the djinn, heaven and earth, air, ether, waters, the light-bearing quality of higher entities, people, animals, birds, plants, and trees—all creations even to the smallest, and the insect, and to the ants, the righteous and the iniquitous, the true and the false, the good and the evil, the pleasant and the unpleasant. If the Word did not exist, neither the just nor the unjust would be cognized, neither true nor false, good nor evil, pleasant nor unpleasant; this Word enables one to distinguish all. Apprehend the proper understanding of the Word."

* * *

"Only when service takes place justly; without sacrifice there will be no justice.

This alone makes service just, but it is needful to wish to cognize service."

"Only when you feel an inner joy at service. He serves not who is in suffering.

Only when one has been filled with joy does service result, but it is needful to cognize joy."

"There is no joy without infiniteness. There is no joy in the finite. Joy is infinity, but it is needful to wish to cognize infinity."

* * *

"Whoever strives to the peace world of fathers, with them will he also dwell. Surrounded by the peace world of fathers, he may be happy. Whoever strives to the peace world of mothers, only to think, will also dwell with them.

Surrounded by the peace world of mothers, he will be happy."

"The truly clear-sighted sees neither deaths nor diseases nor sufferings. The truly clear-sighted sees, and everywhere he attains all."

* * *

"Atman, the sole true reality, is in the heart. This it is that explains the expression: It is in the heart. Day by Day, he who knows this attains the heavenly peace world."

* * *

The lofty spiritual mood in which a Hindu recites the words of the sacred tradition is something not easily forgotten. The poet Tagore, whose sensitive heart is a storehouse of these great rhythms, knows how to evoke all their beauties.

In India, when the verses of the Mahabharata, the Upanishads, and the Puranas are being recited, then there is joy, despite all troubles; and even if the modernization of India is inevitable, the beauty of such sacred poetry will live on forever.

One is, of course, struck by the endless repetitions in the translation of such texts, and yet if one listens to the rhythmic periods of the original, one recognizes that they are an integral part of the melody. Such repetitions are often a way of laying stress on the most important passages. For centuries the Rig-Veda and the other sacred books were transmitted orally, and in this, rhythmic repetition was a great aid to the memory.

If one considers the large number of philosophical and religious periodicals and books now published in India, one is forced to admire a people who care so much for thought and culture. Such a virtue covers many defects, and from the towering Himalayas to the burning South, there are plenty of signs that point in this direction.

From the poorest coolie to the most learned Hindu,

you will always meet with someone ready to converse with you on the most lofty subjects; and after a short time, you will come to realize that every Hindu, whatever be his personal way of life or that of the society to which he belongs, will always prefer to discuss lofty subjects, for these alone to him seem real.

Despite the confusion of today, India still maintains her lofty tradition of Teacher and disciple. The Guru still lives on and the relationship of Guru and disciple is always an edifying one. This noble and conscious cult of the Teacher can hardly be found in other countries. There is nothing servile or belittling in it, no narrowing of outlook or loss of personality, for it is a noble recognition of the Law of Hierarchy.

Even in the details of daily life, the disciples will always respect the Teachers' dignity, a quality that can only be developed by mutual respect.

The Teacher is a father and adviser and a guide in all the events of life.

It is characteristic of the Guru to be concerned about the inner and outer program of his disciple, and the disciples, on their part, have many beautiful expressions that show their deep respect for the Guru. Belittlement, on their part, is inadmissible even in the smallest details, and they will make every endeavor to preserve in their own minds the essential character of the Teacher.

From this mutual understanding, the art of thinking is born, and joy arises around the comprehension of higher things—a joy not confined to palaces and temples, but one that enters the poorest dwelling and transforms the burden of life into something easy.

He who knows India—not as the tourist or sightseer but as one who has come in contact with the people and with the life of the great country—will never forget its charm.

And the heart of India will respond to all genuine sympathy. No words or assurances can compare with the judgment of the heart, which is something steadfast, something that can dive beneath the surface and recognize the essential.

In India, moreover, there is a remarkable psychic awareness; so if you glance at anyone in a distant crowd, he will respond to your attention at once. This we have remarked upon not once or twice but on many occasions.

Such a delicate sense of awareness is not to be acquired by any voluntary training.

It is the heritage of centuries of lofty thought and a natural characteristic of the race. In order to acquire the habit of lofty thought, one must come to prefer it to other ways of thought; in fact, one must rejoice in it, for, as we are told in the Upanishads, it is only through joy that our efforts can become effective.

This inner joy of the heart is something that we have to cultivate and learn how to retain so that it takes up its abode in the heart so that this beneficent joy of the heart becomes a lasting power to disperse all the forces of darkness.

Whether we think of those sublime temples of Southern India, of the grandeur of Chittur and Gwalior and the great strongholds of Rajputana, or the solemn spirit of the Himalayas, everywhere we will find the joy of great thoughts.

On the moonlit Ganges, in the mystery of Benares seen at night, and in the great cadences of the Himalayan waterfalls, we will find the same lofty sense of joy.

In the repetition of such ancient names as Manu, Arjuna, Krishna of the Pandavas—Rishis, heroes, creators and great constructors—we recognize a loving respect for the past.

From the Mother of the World, from the Queen of Peace, we receive this delicate flowerlike joy of the heart.

Marvelous India! Splendid in outer beauty, most beautiful in its secret inner life.

Beautiful, beloved India!

BOOKCASE

O NE recalls an incident: In the office of a certain president are two visitors. The walls of the old room are decorated with massive oak bookcases. Through the glass panels temptingly glow the backs with their rich bindings. Although the bindings are not old, they are heavily gold-leaved. Apparently, here is a lover of books. How splendid that at the head of this undertaking, there is a collector who has not spared money in his tempting bindings.

One of the visitors yields to the temptation of turning the leaves and holding in his hands this treasure of the spirit. The bookcase is apparently unlocked and raising his hand, the booklover attempts to take one of the volumes. But oh, the horror! The entire shelf falls on his head, revealing that these are false bindings without any sign of a book. His most sensitive wish violated, the booklover with trembling hands, replaces upon its shelf, this unworthy imitation: "Let us get away from here soon. Can one expect anything decent from such a clown!" The other visitor smiles: "Here one is punished for loving books because it is a happiness not only to read a good book but even to hold it in one's hands."

How many such false libraries are spread all over the world: and whom do their owners presume to cheat—their own friends or themselves? In this falsification lies hidden an unusually subtle disdain of knowledge and a refined insult toward the book as the witness of human achievement. And not only are the contents of the book being violated but in such falsifications, objectively as well as in words, is being assaulted the very significance of the creation of the spirit.

"Tell me who are your enemies, and I will tell you who you are," said the ancients. One may say, "Show me your bookcase and I will tell you who you are."

One of the most exhausting tasks is the search for a new apartment. But through this involuntary intrusion into numerous dwellings, you undoubtedly discover observations about the facts of life. You pass through numerous apartments of approximate wealth that are filled with furniture. But where is the bookcase? Where is the writing desk? Why are the rooms sometimes overcrowded with such strange, ugly objects, yet these two friends of existence—a writing desk and a bookcase—are lacking? Is there a place to put them? It appears upon examination that a small desk could still be placed somewhere, but the walls are all so figured out that there is no place for a bookcase.

The landlady, noticing your disappointment, points out a small inside closet and with a smile of condescension, indulging your demand, says: "If you have so many books, you can use this closet instead of using it for other domestic things." Thereby you see that the minute measures of the closet appear to be regal for such a luxury as books.

In this regrettably patronizing attitude toward the book you recall the priceless libraries that are apparently thrown out on the street markets. And you once more sorrowfully recall all the stories of how herrings and cucumbers were wrapped in the priceless pages torn from the rarest editions. Then, when you look upon the small bookcase that is being offered to you, and you calculate that only with difficulty could even a hundred volumes fit there, you again hear the "worldly" sages ask you: "Why, then, keep so many books at home?" And they will be only repeating the words of the famous Mussulman conquerer who ordered the most priceless libraries to be destroyed as useless, since it is said that the one Koran comprises everything which is necessary for a human being.

The absence of a writing desk is explained quite definitely by the reminder that a writing desk is supposed to stand in an office. Herein is apparent a definite suggestion that outside the office, there should be no mental occupations and evening relaxations are meant for a hilarious time that should not burden the brain. And thus the so-called relaxations, which should be most priceless hours of accumulation and refinement of consciousness, are dissipated like pearls thrown in the dust of the street.

And thus the book in contemporary usage becomes an object of luxury. The "sane" mind categorizes bibliophiles as luxurious maniacs. The mediocre consciousness altogether unlearns to read, as he even good-naturedly confesses. "I cannot read long books," "I cannot concentrate," "I haven't got the time," says a man on his way to a boxing match or to throw balls into the air or simply too busy himself gossiping about his neighbor.

And there is both time and money to possess houses that are a treasury of knowledge, but the thought about these treasures simply leaves our daily habit. By what do people live? Through many objects. But the realization of this, as well as the beauty of the book itself as a creation, passes out of the life.

So also can one observe the character and the essence of a friend according to the condition in which they return the books loaned to them. It is true that very often you meet with a most careful, a most honorable attitude toward the book, and then you understand why certain volumes remained from the seventeenth and fifteenth centuries. But to one's sorrow more often the books are returned in an irreparably harmed way so that one's soul aches for the desecrated author. To burn a book with something, to turn down the leaves, perhaps to tear away the corner, and sometimes even to cut out the illustration that one likes is not considered a sacrilege. Every librarian will tell you about his grievances not only regarding lost books but also editions mutilated forever.

He who destroys a book reveals the low condition of his consciousness. Truism though this be, let whoever reads it be afraid to soil or tear a book. In the midst of universal crises, material as well as spiritual, the general latitude toward books will be one of the convincing circumstances. Yes, when we will again learn to love a book disinterestedly, as a pure creation of art, and heartily to safeguard it, will be also when also some of the most difficult of life's problems will solve themselves—without discussions, without evil thoughts and clashes. And in our dwellings we will also find a place for a bookcase and for a writing desk as well as for the sacred images, which by their presence remind us about the Highest, the Beautiful, and the Infinite.

Someone may say, "I knew this long ago, this is not new to me." How good it is if he says so; maybe on the strength of that, he will read one more book and his attitude toward these true friends of every home will be more solicitous; and in turn, he will say that which is so known to him and to others. Because it is often about that, which they do not apply, that people say: "I knew that long ago." One must say to them again, "The worse for you."

The books of recent editions have become very meager—both in measure and in their specific contents. The author is seemingly afraid to bore because the publisher dins into his ears about the peculiar demands of the reader.

And suddenly you discover that most of the books are being read by poor people, and the desire of true realizations lives in people who with difficulty earn for themselves the bread of tomorrow. Looking over the almanac of world information, you will, with keen interest, follow the statistic of literacy as well as the number of volumes in public libraries of the world. How inconsistent with many official presentations are distributed the number of books in these National Treasuries. Let us not quote these instructive numbers because *The World Almanac,* a yearly book, is in reach of those who desire to get acquainted with the consistency of these acquisitions. For many people, the figures will contain great surprises.

Because of that, let us not forget that literacy, although undoubtedly a step to culture, is of itself not yet a guarantee of those reading books or their sane cultural application. If one could take another census, namely as to how many of the literate people do not read books, the results would be very instructive. Then also, if from the number of readers would be eliminated the readers of cheap fiction, we would see that the entire number of serious books and editions is supported by a comparatively minute amount of people out of the entire population of the world.

This condition still further demands a careful attitude not only toward serious editions, but also toward those individuals who make out of them a wise and proper application.

Some touching episodes about the loving care of books are not forgotten. Unforgettable is the story of one poor writer who wanted to give to his bride, as a wedding present, what to him was the most valuable thing, a monograph on the creation of an artist who most inspired him. It is also unforgettable when this touching love toward books is kindled independently in the most early youth. A small girl, in a very rich home, carries with difficulty the Bible with illustrations by Doré, too heavy for the child's strength. She is not permitted to take this book, but she takes advantage of the absence of her elders—not for mischief and play but in order again to utilize this moment of freedom to commune with the great Images.

Dear to us are these children, the bearers of the best Images, who, directed by their hearts, independently seek the bookcase in their search for this unchangeable friend of true happiness.

Because Edison spontaneously sought the bookcase, from early childhood he realized how he could benefit humanity. In the community instinct of newspaper work is also expressed a hearty striving toward the spreading of the useful.

Let us also remember the great mind, Ruskin, who so touchingly contributed his first efforts and inspirations toward the great Biblical Epos. Let us remember many glorious ones. Long ago the power of thought was already spoken about as well as the art of thinking. But every art must be developed and nurtured, and shall not the hearth of this sacred art be near a bookcase?

Let us turn to the bookcase not only as to a comforter and guardian but also as to a leader and vitalizer. Do not the consistently creative minds of great thinkers emanate from it? Or vitality? Or does not the resistance to all evil and to all the unprecedented obstacles of existence come from it? And does not creative joy come from it?

REAL VALUES

IN the Nārada Śilpa Śāstra, high ordainments about the significance of art have been given:

"We will speak of the manner of construction of the art gallery. According to Usinara, the art gallery is to be erected in the central part of the city, on a site where four roads cross, in front of palaces and houses or in the center of the main street."

"Pictures are to be such as to captivate our minds and give joy to our eyes. They must be of several colors, brilliant with various color shades. . . ."

"Divine Nārada says that we will speak here of the manner of decoration by painting. According to Usinara, painting is for the pleasure of the gods, for the satisfaction of the presiding deity of the building, and also for beauty."

Thus spoke Nārada.

And in another age, in other expressions, but similarly uplifting, Leonardo da Vinci praises the great meaning of art. The same solemn homage we find amid the Chinese classics, in Japan, in Persia, and everywhere in the world; this is told by the best people in the highest terms.

"Art is not destruction. In art is contained the seed of construction, not destruction. This was felt always, even in those days when everything was ignorance. To the sounds of Orpheus's lyre, entire cities were built. Despite the as-yet-unrefined appreciation of art by the public, everyone says: "Art is the reconciliation with life." This is true. A real creation of art has within itself something soothing and reconciling."

"Art is the reconciliation with life."

"Art is the introduction into the soul of harmony and order, not of confusion and discord."

Thus, almost a hundred years ago, the great men of Russian literature—Gogol and Zhukovsky—corresponded with each other. Both illustrious writers were known for their unusually broad appreciation of art, and, therefore, the words quoted above have a never-fading significance. One must only remember how these two great writers have beautifully expressed themselves in appreciation of the various domains of art. Only broad thinking and an experienced outlook can come to such enlightening and convincing conclusions.

In the essays and letters of these writers, one may find the most touching descriptions of beautiful works of art, ancient as well as modern. One can always rejoice when in any country the people respond with equal love to both the art of antiquity and modern art. He who would show contempt for the past would only disclose himself as an ignoramus. And in the same light would appear he who showed no attention to his contemporary searchings.

Truly, it is impossible to lock oneself forever in grandfather's room. With what indignation one looks at the profanity manifested by those who disparagingly speak of the beloved treasures carried over from beautiful past ages.

Precisely, in limitless art one can study the best observations upon the state of human consciousness. The refinement of consciousness will first of all resound upon all domains of art. In all branches of art and craftsmanship, a broad consciousness will notice an element of true creativeness. After all, art is limitless, and creation realized or hidden, secret, accomplished, or unfinished penetrates everywhere.

Precisely, art secures the high quality of every production. Today the newspapers are laughing that in Pisa a new bridge has just collapsed; whereas the old bridge, constructed six hundred years ago, still stands unharmed. I was also told recently of the similar strength of old Turkish bridges, which withstood even the onslaught of modern artillery fire. In the last earthquake of India and Nepal, the modern buildings have greatly suffered, while the ancient temples have withstood the strain.

One can enumerate endless examples of the triumph of high quality in many ancient arts of the past. We remember with what ease modern colors can be removed from ancient, recently restored paintings. And not only does the difference of age play its part, but the cause lies in the disappearance of the quality of many productions. One dreads to think what will remain in the future of some of the modern creations.

At present, one is moved to emphasize once more that we have received from antiquity much evidence of the facts of how beautiful is the combination of quality and creativeness. It is most inspiring to witness that quality has made it possible for great creations to survive for long ages. We thank the old masters that their methods of work have stood so long and have given to so many people happiness and new inspiration. But when you think of the paths of the protection of cultural treasures, then you especially often meet and come close to the concept of quality. When studying ancient qualities, it will be easier for us to plan our modern buildings so that they can withstand the many calamities of the future, not lose their beauty.

Without exaggeration, the treasures of culture are the stronghold of a nation. The entire upbuilding—all enlightenment, all spiritual inspiration, all happiness and salvation—will be born upon the foundations of cultural treasures. At first let us realize and safeguard culture, and then the designs on the banknotes of the country will also become attractive. Along the innumerable paths of communication, creativeness will surge forward in all its noble multiformity.

Likewise, it will not be an exaggeration to say that the language of the heart has many times proved in the history of mankind most convincing and attractive as well as unifying. Not only are the names of Apollonius, Rubens, Velasquez, and many others immortalized in art but also their unforgettable advice in the field of statesmanship. Objects of art themselves have, many a time, been the best ambassadors, introducing peace and friendship. We already have pointed out that the exchange of art treasures even prevented misunderstandings and was ahead of verbal agreements. If the world, according to Plato, is ruled by ideas, then noble seeds of art will always be that beneficial sowing, which will give the best, well-remembered harvest. Therefore, it will not be commonplace to affirm again and again the wide meaning of art and the true value of the beautiful. Thus let us safeguard everything that is beautiful with all the care of our heart.

For the establishment of our Pact for the Protection of Cultural Treasures, first of all, one has to acquaint oneself with the history of the origin of the Red Cross. The founder of this noble idea, the famous Swiss philanthropist, H. Dunant, and his self-sacrificing friends, for seventeen years have tirelessly knocked at the hearts of mankind in order to tell of the undeferrability of such a humanitarian project. Everyone should remember the history of the Red Cross, which had so many troubles and difficulties. Likewise, in the question of the protection of art treasures, let us always keep in mind that these great treasures are being destroyed not only during times of war but also during the manifestation of every human ignorance. Alone, the protection of cultural treasures will awaken many dormant paths of creativeness and entire countries will again remember that therein lies their strength and unconquerable dignity and value.

Let us always remember how beautifully such great men of India, Vivekananda and Tagore, spoke about art.

Said Vivekananda: "Don't you see? I am, above all, a poet."— "That man cannot be truly religious who has not the faculty of feeling the beauty and grandeur of art."— "Non-appreciation of art is crass ignorance."

Rabindranath Tagore concluded his article *What Is Art?* with the words: "In art the person in us is sending its answer to the Supreme Person, who reveals Himself to us in a world of endless beauty across the lightless world of facts." Who else now could define art better than this glorious poet of India!

In *Leaves of Morya's Garden*, Book One, we read:

"Pure art is the true expression of the radiant Spirit. Through art, you gain the Light!"

MYSTERIES

ON the Karakorum Pass, at nineteen thousand five hundred feet, on this highway, the highest in the world, the groom Goorban began to question me:

"What is it that has been secreted in these heights? It must be that a great treasure has been hidden hereabouts, as the way to this place is surely arduous. Having traversed all the passes, one may chance upon a smooth vault. Something tinkles under the horses' hooves. It must be that here are great secrets, but we do not know the entry-way to them. When will there be writings in books that reveal what has been hidden away, and where?"

All around this majestic Karakorum Pass, the white peaks glistened dazzlingly. All round us without a break rose a most brilliant scintillation. On the path itself, as if for a reminder, lay a great quantity of whitened bones. Were not some of these wayfarers going for treasures? Indeed, countless caravans have crossed the Karakorum for riches.

Here I am reminded of another tradition concerning a treasure. In Italy, at Orvieto, they related a remarkable legend to me about hidden artistic treasures. The story concerned either Duccio himself or one of his contemporaries. It was told in a lofty style that goes so well with the mellifluous Italian language.

"Just as it is nowadays, in olden times, the best artists were not always understood. For the beclouded eye, it has been difficult to evaluate forms, especially lofty ones. People have demanded nothing but the observance of old rules, and beauty has not often been accessible to them. It thus happened with the great artist of whom we are speaking. His best pictures, instead of exaltingly touching the hearts of people, were subjected to condemnation and mockery. For a long time, the artist endured this unjust attitude toward himself.

"In divine ecstasy he continued to create many masterpieces. Once he depicted a marvelous Madonna, but the envious prevented the hanging of this image in its predestined place. And this happened not once or twice, but several times. When the viper begins to creep in, it invades both palace and hovel.

"But the artist, made wiser and knowing the madness of the crowd was not distressed. He said: 'It has been given the bird to sing, and to me has been given the power to glorify lofty forms. As long as the bird lives it fills God's world with song. And so while I am alive, I shall also glorify it. Since the envious and the ignorant put obstacles in the way of my works, I shall not lead the evil ones into worse bitterness of heart. I shall collect the pictures rejected by them. I shall store them securely in oaken chests and, availing myself of the goodwill of my friend the abbot, I shall hide them in the deep cellars of the monastery. When the ordained day shall come, future generations will discover them. If, by the will of the Creator they must remain hidden, let it be so!'

"From this time on, people thought that the great artist had ceased painting. But hearing these suppositions, he only smiled, because henceforth he was not laboring for the sake of the people's joy, but for a higher beauty. And so, we do not know where this priceless treasure is preserved."

"No one knows in precisely what monastery, in what secret vaults, the artist concealed his creations. True, in certain cloisters, old paintings have been found in crypts, but these have been found singly; they were not purposefully deposited there, and therefore could not be the treasure intentionally hidden by the great artist. Indeed in the underground vaults they continue to sing 'Gloria in Excelsis', but searchers have not been fortunate enough to find what was indicated by the artist himself. Certainly we have many monasteries and still more temples and castles that lie in ruins. Who knows, perhaps the tradition relates to one of these remains, already destroyed and razed by time.

"But have you been assured that this treasure is hidden within the boundaries of Italy?" asked one of the listeners.

"Of course even in remote times people were going to other countries. May it not be that these treasures have likewise been unexpectedly dispersed, or rather, preserved in different countries?" Another person added: "It may be that this story does not at all refer to a single master. Of course human practices are often repeated. Consequently, we find in history repetitions of human wanderings and ascents."

When we reached the middle of the Karakorum Pass, the groom Goorban said to me: "Give me a couple of rupees. I will bury them here. Let us too add to the great treasures."

I asked him: "Then do you think that treasures have been collected together there below? He looked surprised, even frightened. "But does the sahib not know? Even to us lowly people it is known that there, deep down, are extensive underground vaults. In them have been gathered treasures from the beginning of the world. There are also great guardians. Some have been fortunate enough to see how, from the hidden entry-ways, come tall white men, who then again withdraw underground. Sometimes they appear with torches, and many caravaneers know these fires. These subterranean beings do no evil. They even help people.

"I know, for a fact, that one local boy was lost from his caravan in a snowstorm and covered his head in despair. Then it seemed to him that someone was moving around him. He looked around in the darkness but there appeared no horse, no man—he saw nothing. Yet, when he put his hand in his pocket, he found a handful of gold pieces.

Thus do the great dwellers of the mountains help miserable people in misfortune."

And again the stories came to mind about the secret magnets established by the followers of the great philosopher and traveler, Apollonius of Tyana.

It is said that in definite places where it had been ordained that new states be built up or great cities erected, or that great discoveries and revelations should take place, there, on all such sites were implanted portions of a giant meteor, sent from the distant luminaries.

There has even been a custom of testifying to the truth of statements by reference to such ordained places. Deponents would say: "What I have said is as true as the fact that on a certain site has been placed such and such..."

The groom Goorban again raised the question: "Why do you foreigners who know so much not find the entryway into the underground kingdom? You know how to do everything and boast of knowing everything, and yet you do not enter into the secrets which are guarded by the great fire!"

> "Man lives in mysteries,
> and these are numberless!"

THE MUSIC OF THE SPHERES

WOULD you restrain the Symphony of the Spheres? Would you bid the thunders of heaven to cease? Would you still the waterfalls and the whirlwinds? Would you command silence of the birds or prohibit the call of the stag? Would you deaden all human song? Would you mute the divine canticles and harmonies? What terror would prevail on earth without the Supreme Sounds! One may not even imagine what would transpire in nature, since sound and light are inalienably united. But fortunately no one can affect this devastating barbarism, since no one's forces can touch the Symphony of the Spheres which shall ring out and exalt the human spirit towards new creations. How many beautiful legends from the most remote times confirm the significance of the divine harmonies! As a symbol for all generations, the myth of Orpheus, who enchanted beasts and all living things with his celestial music has been cited. Even serpents lose their venomous intent before music, and the wild yak becomes calm and yields her milk to those who approach her with song.

It is instructive to notice how many beautiful human achievements would have remained incomplete if unaccompanied by the inspiration of song and music. Without the trumpet call, the walls of Jericho would not have fallen. Finally there is no home nor hut from which sound, as exalting and evoking harmony, may be excluded. We call the book, the friend of the home; we raise our eyes through the contemplation of superb lines and colors. Should we not, then, consider the harmony of the sound as our guide to the highest worlds? It is impossible to conceive of a temple without the harmony of voice or instruments. And King David, the Psalmist, composed his psalms with the thought of their rendition with instruments or voice. Not for the silent bookshelf did the Psalmist King create his invoking and instructive psalms. Not by accident, truly, is sound emphasized in the Bible and in other ancient writings. What can so greatly touch the human heart; what will make it immediately finer and more compassionate, completely broader in the span of receptivity? The expansion of the heart as the all-manifest understanding and the broadest striving engender creativeness in all manifestations.

My young Friends! I speak to you in the same language as to your elders, because your hearts are, if not more, equally open to the Beautiful. By your ingenuousness, your pure smile of joy, you often approach and enter with unusual ease into the Palaces of Beauty. Always, then, whenever you think of the beautiful harmony, of exalting music, always then let your hearts throb more vigorously, pre-sensing that other wondrous Gates are open for you which will lead out to a finer highway for your life's journey. Naturally, you love music. Continue not only to love it but constantly refine your understanding and approach to it. Perceive its meaning more personally; it will reveal your creativeness, will nurture your hearts and make accessible that which, lacking harmony and sound, would perhaps remain ever dormant. Regard music as the "open sesame" of your heart; and what can be more necessary, more beautiful, than a heart infinite in its power and its containment?

Each of us recalls the wonderful poem, "Beda, the Preacher," in which the stones in chorus thundered out their response to his call. If stones can concur and proclaim in harmonious chorus, will men be lower than stones? Are they only fit to quarrel and in contradiction, to mumble the unnecessary? A beautiful symphony unites human hearts. People become not merely listeners, but in their hearts they become partakers of the beautiful act.

And this uplifting call leads them to achievement and to better expressions of life.

To you, my Friends, I send my thoughts for achievement, to those best manifestations of life to which each of you are destined and which only inexcusable neglect can leave unexpressed. Under the best sounds, in sorrow, in labor and in joy, hasten to the predestined Light!

* * *

I remember in Kuchar in Central Asia, somebody told us a beautiful tale about the perfection of Art. In the sand, that hide the buried city of Kuchar, we were amazed to hear such a living tradition, which uplifts art:

"A certain artist was once in need of money and took his painting to a moneylender. The latter was not at home and only a boy was there. This boy gave the artist a very large sum for the painting.

When the money lender returned home, he was furious and shouted to the boy: "Fool, for these butterflies, fruits and vegetables you gave such an enormous sum!" and he discharged the boy.

When the term was due, the artist returned to the money lender's surprise with the money and demanded his painting back. When the money lender gave him the painting, the artist exclaimed: "This is not my painting, where are the butterflies?" The money lender was indeed horrified to see that the butterflies had disappeared and only the fruit and vegetables remained on the painting The artist then told to the money lender: "You discharged the boy and insulted him, but only he can help you in your plight. Call him back at once". The money lender had no other way out but to search for the boy and when the latter came, he said: "Now it is winter and the butterflies come only in the summer time. Place the painting near the fire, and we shall see the butterflies return". And so it was. It appeared that the paint was put on the canvas with such skill and special knowledge of colors, that during the cold weather these colors disappeared and became visible only when it got warm again, following the perfection of nature."

Thus beautifully speak these remote people glorifying the standards of Art.

Remember the sense of the Beautiful. Keep your enthusiasm, and develop creative thought—such thought is the chief thing—that power of thought is the real possibility and it is the most practical advice to have pure thoughts.

*   *   *

Lovingly does Asia guard the traditions about the perfection of quality, which resounds with Cosmos.

Amidst the vast uplands of the Gobi we heard an uplifting song. A lonely bard—a Mongol— sitting on a hillock, callingly addressed himself to the dawn. When we came nearer, the Mongol became silent. We asked him to repeat his beautiful tune. But he refused: "only to the desert is this Song of Shambhala sounded."

"*Neti, neti*" says the Hindu of the Unutterable—Ineffable. And will he ever tell you the name of his Guru? The Unspeakable sounds in the heart.

In the sacred fires of the heart will the Music of the Spheres resound, as the highest leading inspiration.

II

HEROES OF CULTURE

HEROES

IN the newspaper *Isvestya* (Moscow, 1944), Elena Bragantzeva writes about the preservation of the Novgorod treasures of antiquity. She also mentions Tamara Konstantinova, who has devoted a great deal of work, in a general way, for the people. Verily, the saving of the people's heritage during the war is a true achievement. The names of such workers must be broadly recorded and preserved for posterity. Let all those be revered who, with danger to their lives, labor for the saving and preservation of cultural treasures. And if someone was not quick enough to understand how to save the national heritage in time, let his unfortunate name also be recorded.

We read in the newspapers about many volunteers who helped in the work of preservation of national treasures. These volunteers comprise a true legion of honor. Let all these valued workers be honored, as Heroes of Culture. Mother—the Heroine, this is a valorous distinction, but the Hero of Culture will also he recorded with reverence in the memory of the nation.

The war heroes are justly honored. The people will take pride in their names, knowing how much self-sacrifice was written into the pages of world history by the Russian Army. How many obstacles were conquered for the glory of the Motherland! A great epic was created, to be remembered by future generations. Victory, victory! And what an unusual victory of a whole people which brought forth a host of heroes.

Alongside the war heroes there have arisen heroes of labor, who have given their strength also for the glorious victory. Side by side with them also labored the heroes of Culture—saviors of the national heritage. And among them will be many unknown heroes, who cared greatly about the protection of the cultural treasures. We have heard about many of them, but there are a great many more who have not yet been revealed. However, they will be found and the nation will bow to them.

Recently, Yakovlev spoke beautifully to the young people about the restoration of the art works. The architects are already working to rebuild the cities. It is astonishing to observe how much has been already restored in that tremendous national uprising.

Amidst pain and sorrow a people molds new glory for its beloved country. Heroes of war, heroes of labor, heroines—mothers, heroes of Culture, a great unconquerable host of heroes!

Thus people are again in a heroic period of construction. Just we have received from Moscow the magazine *Slaviane* with a magnificent article by the famous architect Stchussev about speedy reconstruction of the cities destroyed by German vandalism. What a glorious incessant work! Untiring heroes!

Verily, in all countries real heroes are needed. War Armageddon is over, but now an Armageddon of Culture is raging. All culture warriors should be ready for a common co-operative work.

For twenty-two years we have been connected with India and can speak about cultural needs of this great country. In India a glorious Renaissance of Art, Science and Culture is approaching and people should be prepared to meet this benevolent turn of Evolution. Nowadays after a victorious war all cultural needs have become apparent and should be fostered.

In the sacred traditions of Bharata, Art and Knowledge were venerated as moving powers of the Nation. The same beautiful tradition should be upheld just now when the whole world is searching for the best ways towards a Renaissance. The needs of the young generation should be, met by all means.

The centers of Culture would be deeply welcomed by artists and scientists by all cultural workers. For the young generation such Centers will become indispensable. Artists have no exhibition Hall, but without encouragement Art cannot grow—on ice there are no flowers. There must be Halls for lectures. Museums should grow not only as museums of Archeology, but also of contemporary Art. The Libraries should be enriched by best editions, thus helping the young writers. Unlimited is the sacred plow-field of Culture. The blessed future can grow only on cultural unity. Not only in big cities but even in rural areas such centers could be started. From a small corn grows a mighty oak. An endless host of heroes is needed for such strongholds of Culture. Humanity has a Red Cross for physical welfare, but even more needed is the Red Cross of Culture.

DEFENSE OF VALUES

SPEAKING of the Pact for the preservation of artistic and scientific treasures, I agree with you that all conventional leagues and "uncultured non-cooperations," as Masaryk called them, lead to nothing. From this standpoint, pacts are nothing more than scraps of paper. My idea, however, is very different. For a long time I have been a member of the French Red Cross, having been elected a life member, so I am well aware of the history of this admirable institution from the day of its of its founding by H. Dunant.

I remember the irony and derision that hailed his idea, and this great Swiss was labeled utopian and mocked for his impracticable ideas.

Seventeen years of steady labor were required before he was able to realize his humanitarian scheme, and what seemed impossible was eventually realized.

Even today, you will find people who take an evil pleasure in stating that Italian bombs recently destroyed Red Cross hospitals. Barbarous incidents, however, do not affect the lofty ideals of the Red Cross. One can spit at and insult divine images, but this is not likely to change their character. When Millet's *Angelus* was disfigured by vandals, it did not lose its significance.

My idea concerning the preservation of artistic and scientific treasures aims at creating an international impulse to protect all that is precious and valuable to life.

If the Red Cross sign recalls humanitarianism, then a similar sign ought to remind mankind of its cultural treasures.

From his early school years and throughout all of his social manifestations, man should have a clear conception of the significance and the importance of art and science.

Pictorial impressions are the most lasting and decisive. If children, then, are taught from their early years to respect the Red Cross of Culture, then their consciousness is much more likely to rise to a higher plane. In our correspondence on such matters, we have received many interesting suggestions. In Paris, the well-known literary paper—*Les Nouvelles littéraires*—has invited correspondence on the subject and will be publishing letters from General Gamelin, Paul Jameau, Ugo Oggetti, Philadelphus, and other prominent people. The subject was brought to the fore in an article by our friend De la Pradelle concerning the preservation of works of art in times of war. A professor once wrote to me: "You rouse me and make me ashamed of myself, and leave no room for pessimism and dejection." If a man feels ashamed, then it means that he has begun to ponder over the value of art and science, which we should all do, morning, noon, and night. My effort then has been to stimulate thought toward a higher level rather than argue over scraps of paper.

If, as in the case of H. Dunant, we must put up with all sorts of abuse, this will not discourage us. The archives of literature and the opinions of all sorts of individuals point to endless strife and effort in this direction. Humanity is a long way from peace; nevertheless, in all lands people today aspire toward the "peace of all the world."

This would seem to be a sublime utopia, and yet the human heart will never pray for war, even though this remains the infamous condition of our time.

Space is filled with prayers for the peace of the whole world, and in this saturation of space, there is light and optimism. And if it is not to be for us today, then let us hope that it will be for the humanity that is to come, and that we have been told to love. There may be very different opinions as to the present state of mankind, and one can look upon scientific progress with pessimism or optimism.

Currently, however, malice and hatred are pouring up from the pit of darkness, and it is very difficult for people to see clearly. The weak in spirit do not understand how those who are predisposed to right conduct are often kept apart by trifling prejudices, which we ought to overcome by setting an example to the younger generation. Not so much time now remains for us to labor in this world and to set forth all we have learned from our contact with the most varied types of people.

Suspicion, belittlement, and indifference there cannot be where the heart is concerned, and so, let us continue to express the desires of the heart.

In all of us there is a fund of precious recollection that can be of use in all circumstances. You know that I and all of us have to undergo slander. Not long ago a friend wrote from Paris to say that certain people had invented all sorts of fictions about me, going as far as to allege that I did not paint my pictures. All this, however, has no effect because truth is a thing that will come out. Long ago it was said, "Grief today, tomorrow joy."

VANDALISM

CULTURE and Peace—the most sacred goal of Humanity! In the days of great confusion, both material and spiritual, the disturbed spirit strives to these radiant strongholds. But we should not unite only abstractly in the name of these regenerating conceptions. According to our abilities, each in their own field should bring them into actual surrounding life, as the most necessary and undeferrable.

For forty years, we have been trying to combat vandalism. At our Peace Pact meeting in 1929, we proposed a special Banner of Peace for the protection of all cultural treasures. Committees for promoting the Peace Pact were elected in New York. An international union for the Pact was established with its central seat in Bruges, where a congress for spreading the ideal of Peace through Culture was in session, with the most significant results, proving how close this aim is to the hearts of all the positive people in the world.

From all light-bearing centers should thunder ceaselessly the worldwide call to eliminate the very possibility of wars and create for generations to come new, lofty traditions of the veneration of real cultural treasures. Untiringly unfurling the Banner of Peace everywhere, we, by this, destroy the very physical field for war.

Let us also affirm the World Day of Culture, when simultaneously in all schools and all educational institutions, the world will be reminded of the true treasures of humanity, of creative heroic enthusiasm, of the betterment and adornment of life. For this purpose we have not only to safeguard, by all available means, our cultural heritage, but we must consciously value these treasures, remembering that every contact with them will already ennoble the human spirit.

As we have already witnessed, wars cannot be stopped by interdicts, nor can malice nor falsehood be prohibited. But undeferrably, patiently striving to the highest treasures of humanity, we may make these issues of darkness altogether inadmissible, as breeds the progeny of crass ignorance. The ennobled expanded consciousness, having contacted the realm of culture will naturally enter the path of peaceful constructiveness, discarding as shameful rubbish all belittlement of human dignity generated by ignorance.

The lists of adherers to the Banner of Peace are already long and glorious. The banner has already been consecrated during the congress in Bruges in the Basilica of the Holy Blood, and by this had been given the sacred oath to introduce it everywhere by all means. Friends from all ends of the world, who have trusted and have saturated space with their heartiest wishes, will not look in vain for the Banner over all the shrines of real treasures. Every day brings new letters, new responses. The election run "for peace" has been filled with precious tokens. Verily peace and culture are at present especially and urgently needed.

It is not so much a new law, but the imperative wish, the one panhuman desire, to safeguard the achievements of mankind, which is so badly needed. Every endeavor, even the most evident, requires an active start. For peace and culture one does not need a unanimous worldwide votum. The beautiful principles of the General Good can be affirmed on every scale, still retaining their vital potentiality. Let us wholeheartedly greet all coworkers: "Proceed victoriously, without any delay, with your full abilities along this glorious path!"

Verily, time is short; lose neither a day nor an hour. Kindle the flame of the heart with indomitable enthusiasm. Under the Banner of Peace, let us proceed toward the One Supreme Culture in powerful union as the World League of Culture!

Nefarious German vandalism far superseded the notorious Herostratus, who enlisted his name in history. More and more we are witnessing innumerable, ugly destructions, and alas, they increase. Humanity does not become better, and I recall the sorrowful words of my late friend Rabindranath Tagore in a letter just before his last illness!

"The problem of peace today is the most serious concern with humanity, and our efforts seem so insignificant and futile before the onrush of a new barbarism that is sweeping over the West with an accelerating momentum. The ugly manifestations of naked militarism on all sides forebode an evil future, and I almost lose faith in civilization itself. And we cannot give up our efforts, for that would only hasten the end.

"Today I stand as much perplexed and distressed as you are with regard to the turn of events in the West; we can but hope that the world may emerge but cleaner through this bath of blood. But one must be too daring to risk a prophecy these days.

"Yours is a dedicated life, and I hope you will long be preserved to continue your service to culture and humanity."

Indeed, we cannot give up our efforts. The war of Armageddon is over, but the Armageddon of culture is raging.

Not in the skins of cavemen but in smoking jackets sit these "gentlemen" who, unpunishable for their destructive arrogance and ignorance, shamefully exclaim, "To hell with culture!" There is many a Herostratus! We set down the name of a maniac as a most shameful stigma, but not to burden the pages of history. Criminal savagery turns first of all against the most exalted and perfect creations. Ignorance attempts to disfigure the greatest—therein is the hideous zeal of darkness.

Verily, the most penetrating universal measures are needed in order to renew the traditions of culture. Let us hope, from the depths of our hearts, that the newly formed World League of Culture will truly, universally enlighten all the embittered, bewildered, obscured hearts with a new and benevolent life.

If humanity is to abandon all its highest principles and stake all its hope on sandbags, then it has come to a very sorry pass.

Everything today justifies us and our friends in issuing a call to defend all national treasures. It is said that when the ostrich gets wind of danger, it thrusts its head beneath its wing or in the sand. Natural history is full of such examples, and we might do worse than study the life of ants and bees, which possess superb organization.

In every periodical we look at today, we come across illustrations of barbarous destruction. Such documents will continue to live as a shameful witness of what has been done by the humanity of our times, although the whole of mankind is, of course, not necessarily engrossed in such destruction. But such acts are being perpetrated before the eyes of all, and when we figure the percentage of those who raise their voices to protest, it is not overwhelming. In any street accident you will find four classes of people around you: those who make a genuine effort to help; those who congregate from mere curiosity, others who draw off in fear, and finally, those who take pleasure in the misfortune of others. And with vandalism, it is all the same. Whether active or passive, they are the same uncultured destroyers. Toleration toward evil differs little from evil itself, and it is high time for humanity to give attention to the passive type of vandal. Before our eyes all kinds of destruction are going on, either from the bombs of totalitarian warfare or from human poisoning of one sort or another. It is a question of which sort of poison is the more ruinous—that of poison gas or that which aims at the destruction of culture. In so-called peaceful communities, anti-cultural processes are now taking place on a large scale, while people remain silent or crowds are divided, as in the case of street accidents. At such times, alas, the number of those who exert themselves on behalf of culture is extremely small, while the crowd of those who are curious or malignant takes on huge proportions.

All these curious or evil-minded people try to excuse their conduct, but they are unwilling to reflect that in so doing, they range themselves alongside the vandals.

All who evade joining in the defense of culture enlist in the ranks of passive vandals. In passivity there is always a kind of activity, which can be very dreadful and repulsive, with consequences that may bring about the disintegration of an entire nation.

The passive vandal ought not to imagine that his silence has no effect.

On the contrary, history exposes not only the active vandal but also those who stood by idly and looked on while torture and destruction were being committed.

How heartless, how cruel are all those who feign deafness and remain silent when they ought to cry out.

We have spoken of the defense of everything that helps in the evolution of the human race.

Defense is one thing, but aggression is quite another. We have issued a call not to bury ourselves under sandbags but to counteract destruction through the power of thought, of culture.

Traces of culture are being destroyed, obliterated, and scattered abroad; and in allowing this, mankind has composed a page of history that will look very black in the future.

The doings of such brutal destroyers and torturers will be recorded together with the fact that a vast portion of humanity connived and assisted in such vandalism.

There are many ways of participating in such crimes. One need not launch a bomb oneself from an airplane; there are also those who manufacture bombs and invent arms and engines of destruction. One who stands opposed to cultural undertakings brings on a condition of savagery, destruction, and a distortion of constructive thoughts.

From such premeditated schemes, the dispersal,

dismemberment, and annihilation of whole groups of accumulated treasures can arise. Everyone who, by deed or thought, contributes to such destruction must be included with the vandals who play havoc with the human spirit.

Terrible deeds are going on in the world. Devastating wars are no longer known as wars. The direst destruction goes by the name of "change of policy," while the vandals strut round in new uniforms and trappings, and look upon themselves as the arbiters of destiny.

Does it matter which way man rushes to fratricide and self-destruction? Perhaps we will have a new march composed someday for those who proceed toward criminal vandalism.

Yet there are this enormous majority of curious and malicious onlookers, this odious tribe who fail to understand that they themselves are furthering all sorts of vandalism.

It is horrible to witness how the heirs of Goethe and Schiller have become cruel vandals.

On the first day of the war, we appealed to all the defenders of cultural treasures.

"The thunder of the European war again demands that active attention should be paid to the defense of cultural treasures. A pact to this effect is under consideration by many of the European governments and has already been signed by twenty-one governments of the Americas. No doubt, since military operations have already begun, it is hardly to be expected that any agreement could take place during actual warfare. Yet the activities of our committees should at all times be fruitful. Remembering the position in which the protection of cultural treasures was at the beginning of 1914, we must say that, at present, this important question has definitely been given much more attention by governments and public institutions. Doubtless the activities of our committees have had beneficial influence upon public opinion and have contributed to such an increase of attention. Besides government decrees, public opinion is the first defender of national treasures that have a universal value. During the last great war, we applied our utmost efforts to draw attention to the fact that it is criminal to destroy historical, scientific, and artistic monuments. Then during recent conflagrations, as, for instance, in Spain and China, we happened to hear that our Pact was mentioned and applied in some cases. Also, now all of our committees and groups of friends, to whom the preservation of world treasures is dear, should immediately draw the attention of the public to the importance and urgency of the protection of the creations of human genius. Each one of us has certain opportunities of spreading this panhuman idea. Everyone who has connections with the press or who is a member of some cultural organization should consider it his duty to say, wherever he can, a good and impressive word about the defense of that on which the evolution of humanity is based. On March 24 this year, our committee undertook a series of steps imploring European governments to consider without delay the need of defending cultural treasures. We see now that such an appeal was most timely. Let every cultural worker remember now all of his connections and possibilities in order to strengthen, by all means, public opinion, which is first of all the guardian of world treasures. Friends, act urgently."

Now again we are appealing to all cultural workers:

Friends,

The Armageddon of war is ended, and now humanity must realize and solve the problem of the Armageddon of culture. Under benevolence, let the structure of true, invincible culture be strongly buttressed. Not a shaky civilization that at times forgets about humaneness, but glorious culture—that inextinguishable torch upon the paths of ascent—will be our common goal.

We have already written about a timely rebirth of the Banner of Peace, our Red Cross of Culture. Yes, it is time to speak again about cultural values. This activity is inseparably close to the work of culture. The field of culture is vast, and on such a spacious pasture, all, from small to great, can find application for beneficent endeavor. During recent years, the world has seen so much vandalism, so much savage cruelty! The Red Cross of Culture must glow again.

Recall the great international names that subscribed to and endorsed the Banner of Peace. The archives of our conventions carry indelible and beautiful words that cannot be erased by any vandalism. If timid ones will doubt and will question the possibility of raising again the Banner of Culture, let them know that it will not require overburdening, and that culture is not dependent on wealth.

Fruitful seeds can be sown in one's own circle, in the garden of his best striving. Everyone has access to the printed word and can use this instrument for the Common Good. All dream of peace, of enduring peace, but it will not come through international policing; neither will it be affirmed by "don'ts" and "threats." Peace must be molded first in the human heart, and the heart can develop the capacity for full trust only through culture.

"Peace through Culture" is our constant motto. Events have proven that culture is necessary as a protective shield for humanity. If anyone imagines that a "civilized" man cannot become savage, he is mistaken. A civilized savage is the ugliest spectacle. Therefore, let us again rally around the Banner of Peace. Let us *work*, under the Red Cross of Culture, utilizing every possibility toward the healing of humanity's wounds.

In this endeavor, gather small nuclei throughout the face of the earth. Each such good-creating cell somewhere, somehow will ennoble, will elevate thoughts. They will create new strongholds of culture. The cementing of space for the Common Good is a panacea within reach of everyone. Let your words about culture, about everything beautiful, about that which makes the human heart live, ring out incessantly.

The Armageddon of culture is raging. Beware of vandalism.

Satyam, Shivam, Sundaram.

ADAMANT

TO the sacred ideals of nations in our days, the watch-words, "art and knowledge," have been added with special imperativeness. It is just now that something must be said of the particular significance of these great conceptions, both for the present time and for the future. I address these words to those whose eyes and ears are not yet filled with the rubbish of everyday life, to those whose hearts have not yet been stopped by the lever of the machine called "mechanical civilization."

Art and knowledge! Beauty and wisdom! Of the eternal and still renewed meaning of these conceptions, it is not necessary to speak. When but starting on the path of life, every child already instinctively understands the value of decoration and knowledge. Only later, under the grimace of disfigured life, does this light of the spirit become darkened; while in the kingdom of vulgarity, it has no place and is unknown. Yes, the spirit of the age attains even such monstrousness!

It is not the first time that I have knocked at these gates, and I here again appeal to you:

Among horrors, in the midst of the struggles and the conflicts of the people, the question of knowledge and the question of art are matters of first importance. Do not be astonished. This is not exaggeration; neither is it a plati-tude. It is a decided affirmation.

The question of the relativity of human knowledge has always been much argued. But now, when the whole of mankind has felt directly or indirectly the horrors of war, this question has become a vital one. People have not only become accustomed to think but even to speak without shame about things of which they evidently have not the slightest knowledge. On every hand, men repeat opinions that are altogether unfounded. And such judgments bring great harm into the world, an irreparable harm.

We must admit that during the last few years, European culture has been shaken to its very foundation. In the pursuit of things, the achievement of which has not yet been opened to mankind, the fundamental steps of ascent have been destroyed. Humanity has tried to lay hold of treasures that it has not deserved and so has rent the benevolent veil of the Goddess of Happiness.

Of course, what mankind has not yet attained, it is destined to attain in due time; but how much man will have to suffer to atone for the destruction of the forbidden gates! With what labor and with what self-denial will we have to build up the new bases of culture!

The knowledge that is locked up in libraries or in the brains of teachers again penetrates but little into contemporary life. Again, it fails to give birth to active creative work.

Modern life is filled with the animal demands of the body. We come near to the edge of the terrible magic circle. And the only way of conjuring its dark guardians and escaping from it is through the talisman of true knowledge and beauty.

The time when this will be a necessity is at hand.

Without any false shame, without the contortions of savages, let us confess that we have come very near to barbarism. For confession is already a step toward progress.

It matters not that we still wear European clothes and, following our habit, pronounce special words. But the clothes cover savage impulses, and the meaning of the words pronounced, although they are often great, touching, and uniting, is now obscured. The guidance of knowledge is lost. People have become accustomed to darkness.

More knowledge! More art! There are not enough

of these bases in life, which alone can lead us to the golden age of unity.

The more we know, the more clearly we see our ignorance. But if we know nothing at all, then we cannot even know we are ignorant. And that being so, we have no means of advancement and nothing for which to strive. And then the dark reign of vulgarity is inevitable. The young generations are not prepared to look boldly, with a bright smile, on the blinding radiance of knowledge and beauty. Whence then is the knowledge of the reality of things to come? Whence then are wise mutual relations to arise? Whence is unity to come, that unity that is the true guarantee of steady forward movement? Only on the bases of true beauty and of true knowledge can a sincere understanding between the nations be achieved. And the real guide would be the universal language of knowledge and of the beauty of art. Only these guides can establish that kindly outlook that is so necessary for future creative work.

The path of animosity, roughness, and abuse will lead us nowhere. Along that way nothing can be built. Does not a conscience still remain in human nature? The real being in man still seeks to attain justice.

Away with darkness—let us do away with malice and treachery. Mankind has already felt enough of the hand of darkness.

Let me tell you, and mind you, these are not platitudes, not mere words; I give voice to the convinced seeking of the worker: the only bases of life are art and knowledge.

It is just that in these hard days of labor, in this time of suffering, we must steadily recall these kindly guides. And in our hours of trial, let us confess to them with all the power of our spirit.

You say, "Life is hard. How can we think of knowledge and beauty if we have nothing to live on?" or "We are far away from knowledge and art. We have important business to attend to first."

But I say, You are right, but you are also wrong.

Knowledge and art are not luxuries. Knowledge and art are not idleness. It is time to remember this: They are prayer and the work of the spirit. Do you really think that people pray only when overfed or after excessive drinking, or during the time of careless idleness?

No, men pray in the moments of greatest difficulty. So, too, is this prayer of the spirit most needful when one's whole being is shaken and in want of support, and when it seeks for a wise solution. And wherein lies the stronger support? What will make the spirit shine more brightly?

We do not feel hunger or starvation; we do not shiver because of the cold. We tremble because of the vacillation of our spirit, because of distrust, because of unfounded expectations.

Let us remember how often when working, we have forgotten about food, have left unnoticed the wind, the cold, the heat. Our intent spirit wrapped us in an impenetrable veil.

"The weapon divideth it not, the fire burneth it not, the water corrupteth it not, the wind drieth it not away; for it is indivisible, inconsumable, incorruptible and is not to be dried away; it is eternal, universal, permanent, immovable. . . . Some regard the indwelling spirit as a wonder, whilst some speak and others hear of it with astonishment; but no one realizes it, although he may have heard it described." (*Bhagavad Gita*, Ch. II)[*]

Of what does the great wisdom of all ages and all nations speak? It speaks of the human spirit. Penetrate in thought into the deep significance of these words and into the meaning of your life. You know not the limits to the power of the spirit. You do not know over what impassable obstacles your spirit bears you, but some day you will awake, unharmed and everlastingly regenerated. And when life is hard and weary, and there seems to be no

---

[*] *The Bhagavad-gita, the book of devotion: dialogue between Krishna, lord of devotion, and Arjuna, prince of India.* William Q. Judge (Translator). 10th ed. Los Angeles, California: United Lodge of Theosophists, 1920, p.13.

way out, do you not feel that some helper, your own divine spirit, is speeding to your aid? But his path is long and your faintheartedness is swift. Yet does the helper come, bringing you both the 'sword of courage' and the 'smile of daring.' We have heard of a family that in despair put an end to their lives with fumes of charcoal. Now this was intolerably fainthearted. When the coming victory of the spirit arrives, will not they who have fled without orders suffer fearfully because they did not apply their labor as they should have applied it? It matters not what labor. The drowning man fights against the flood by all possible means. And if his spirit is strong, then the strength of his body will increase without measure.

But by what means will you call forth your spirit? By what means will you lay bare that which in man is buried under the fragments of his everyday life? Again and again I repeat: by the beauty of art, by the depth of knowledge. In them and in them alone are contained the victorious conjurations of the spirit. And the purified spirit will show you what knowledge is true, what art is real. I am assured that you will be able to call your spirit to your aid. That spirit, your guide, will show you the best paths. It will lead you to joy and victory. But even to victory, it will lead you by a lofty path whose steps are bound together by knowledge and beauty alone. . . . An arduous trial awaits the whole world: the trial by assimilation of truth. After the medieval trials by fire, water, and iron, now comes the trial by assimilation of truth. But if the power of the spirit upheld men against fire and iron, then will that same power also raise them up the steps of knowledge and beauty. But this test is more severe than the trials of antiquity. Prepare to achieve! Prepare for that achievement that is a matter of daily life. Meanwhile have care for everything that serves to advance the perception of truth. Approach with special gratitude all that shows forth the stages of beauty. At this time, all this is especially difficult.

But adamant-like stands Beauty.

URGENT PROBLEMS

"A NEW law forbids any loan of Italy's art." (*New York Times*, January 28, 1940). We deeply appreciate this law. In connection with it, I remember my address to the Conference of Experts, which took place in Rome in October 1930. Some excerpts are also absolutely urgent now.

In the course of the last few years, the safeguarding of artistic treasures has begun to be organized according to new methods that must be examined with attention and also with prudence. The introduction of the X-ray—that new and powerful factor in the study of works of art—causes us to admire the new possibilities placed at our disposal by science for the search of truth, but it also obliges us to wonder whether this method will not produce certain effects on the colors as much as on the other elements of works of art. No one can doubt that powerful X-rays produce consequences that may be either beneficial or destructive. But the highest authorities are unable to certify that this energy, applied to works of art, will remain neutral and without effect. The time that has passed since the introduction of X-rays is too short to permit a definite conclusion as to their effects. Thus, although no one had the intention of inventing varnish or pigments that would be harmful, yet various effects of these "perfections" are revealed after several centuries as bringing harm to the magnificent productions of human genius.

Certainly it does not follow that we should take a definite stand for the old methods without searching for new means of approaching the truth. Everything must progress.

Among the enterprises that are most useful in this respect, we count, for example, the laboratory that is now being organized at the Louvre, and where, thanks to the energy and gracious initiative of M. Henri Verne, new scientific methods can be determined and verified. I believe that I should salute here this extremely useful enterprise, by expressing the hope that similar laboratories, organized in accordance with the most recent scientific principles, be installed in all countries in order to study the effects of local climates and pigmentations as well as the technical methods in use, which have been adapted to the particular conditions of each place. It is important in this respect for the laboratories in question to coordinate their work and exchange the results of their experiments. It is also necessary that researches of long duration be undertaken. Undoubtedly, one human life would not suffice for the study of certain results of these experiments; but for the good of the future, it would be necessary, beginning now, to commence coordinated research work that others would continue until a very far-distant time.

We must reconcile modern discoveries with the experience of past ages brought down to us by the works preserved and also take into consideration the preparatory works of the old masters—for example, the methods by which the oil used for painting was purified during a period of several years, the preparation of varnish and "olifs" by the primitives and monographers, and finally, the choice of woods for the panels, not to speak of colors. Still, this obliges us to fix our attention on the qualities of ancient methods, allied to modern improvements.

If the conference adopts the principle of coordinating artistic research laboratories affiliated with museums, I could propose that our museum joins in this useful and necessary cooperation. The idea of intellectual cooperation in itself indicates that this international institution could proceed to the revision and to the exchange of research work and of its results. Thus, with the end of serving future generations, still another fertile collaboration would be realized.

In addition, aside from the perfecting of technical methods, it is certainly necessary to take into consideration another essential question, that of the exchange of works of art and especially the exchange of exhibitions of older creations.

This question causes contradictory thoughts to arise.

On the one hand, everyone understands that a better international agreement can be developed on the basis of art and science. Nothing in this world can take the place of these forces of peaceful enthusiasm and cordial fervor. But on the other hand, one must not lose sight of the considerable *risks* and *dangers* that the transportation of works of art entails. Without counting the danger of the transportation itself, which is great in spite of the most careful precautions, we know that works of art, like living organisms, are divided into "migrators" and "sedentaries." Strange though it may seem, works that are "migrators," by the will of Destiny, support the perils of travel much more easily than those that have passed centuries in one fixed place, without risking the hazards of life. How often have I seen manifested, with sudden malignancy following a transfer, an "illness," which under other conditions would not have occurred. Everyone knows the surprises occasioned by the transporting of a work across the ocean. Even with thick boards, in spite of the most careful wrapping, the linings become bloated and crack. The original coating heaves up and often imposes on the operation, always undesirable, of transferring the painting to a canvas. All linings (*maroufles*) frequently become bloated. Similar injuries also ruin sculptured woods and ivories. These are the risks that no insurance can cover. Also, without diminishing in the least degree the great task of art, whose role consists in being the intermediate agent between the peoples of the world, it is necessary to think of the intensification and of the rationalization of traveling, rather than of increasing the transporting of works of art into different climates, which breaks in some way the secular vibrations that surround the work of art.

All those who have charge of artistic treasures know that painful feeling that comes over them in seeing the injuries suffered by works confided to their care. We know how many just regrets arise following each transfer of works of art. Undoubtedly, particular care and judicious choosing, not only in accordance with their quality but also in accordance with their physical nature can, to a certain degree, keep the productions of genius from the perils of these long voyages.

The coordination of the researches organized by museum laboratories, as discussed above, would be useful in all respects, and it would particularly please me to know the opinion of the conference on this point, which our institutions would be happy to study in view of their imminent realization.

Art should be protected by all means. Armageddon is roaring.

Art and knowledge are the cornerstones of evolution. Art and science are always needed, but in our days of Armageddon, they must be especially guarded by all the powers of our hearts. It is a great mistake to think that during troubled times culture can be disregarded. On the contrary, the need of culture is especially felt in times of war and human misunderstandings; outside of art, religion is inaccessible; outside of art, the spirit of nationality is lost; outside of art, science is dark. This is not a utopia. The history of humanity gives innumerable examples of art being the great beacon of light in times of calamity. Scientists assert that color and sound are a panacea. By beauty and harmony even wild beasts were tamed. Let the sacred flute of Sri Krishna resound again! Let us visualize that peace in which the majestic frescoes of Ajanta were created! In times of war, let us think of future peace, affirmed by creativeness, labor, and beauty. Traveling through blessed India, we once passed along a road in the shadow of mighty chinars. Our guide told us,

"The great Emperor Akbar thought of the future travelers who would be sheltered by these beautiful trees. He looked into the future." "To regard the Beautiful means to improve," said Plato. "Man becomes that of which he thinks," preordained the Upanishads.

MARIA TENISHEVA

THROUGHOUT the history of mankind, periods of destruction and denial have always been succeeded by those of construction. In these latter, the "constructors" of all ages and nations have found themselves on the same side.

Men destroyed, squandered, with nothing to substitute for what they laid waste. But it is said, "Do not destroy the temple unless you can erect a new one in its place."

The names of the squanderers and of the destroyers have either been swallowed by the darkness of oblivion or have become dreadful phantoms, terrifying new generations.

But in times of reconstruction, the names of those who took up the task of building anew, mindful of the future, will be linked together in one endless chain. And humanity will always look back at them with a sigh of refuge in the hope for evolution. Varied are their names; far divided are they by countless centuries; diverse are the fields on which they wielded their invincible weapons for the progress of humanity; yet in spite of all these differences, they possess the same qualities.

Indefatigability, fearlessness, a thirst for knowledge, tolerance, and a capacity for enlightened labor—such are the qualities of the seekers for truth. There is still another quality that unites more closely these varied phenomena: that difficulty of attainment, inherent in all progressive movements, that falls to the lot of these toilers whose aim is to bring spiritual light to the Universe.

It is a custom to speak lightly of the "martyrs of science, the martyrs of creative work, the martyrs of constructive work, the martyrs of the seeking spirit." These words are uttered as calmly as a discussion of one's daily diet or conventional habits, as though this martyrdom had become indispensable and immutable. The adherents of coarseness and vulgarity warn their children, "Why should you become martyrs, when, thanks to our efforts, we can offer you an easy life and an appetite unspoiled by burdensome thoughts? See how hard it is for the seekers for truth; only a very few of them walk unwounded along the precipice of life. You are our children, and therefore you must assume the same undisturbed position in the cemetery that we have earned by our desire for tranquility."

Yet beyond all question, it is this very tranquility that comprises the most terrible death because that which lives never demands quiescence but, on the contrary, lives in an eternal pulsation of self-perfection.

Maria Klaudievna Tenisheva—a "constructor" and a collector—has left us.

Her life could have been calm and untroubled. Conforming to the established standards, she could have safely invested her capital in various countries and found herself, in the end, among those who take no part in the violent commotions of humanity and live peacefully until a natural death overtakes them.

But a longing for knowledge and beauty, and an irresistible urge to create and to build kept Maria Tenisheva away from the still waters. She never experienced deadly tranquility. She yearned to know, to create, to go forward.

Perhaps those who only met Maria Tenisheva amid the conventional smiles of social life would disagree with me. For the spirit of seeking was so tense and so deeply rooted within her that its essence came to the surface only on rare occasions. To know that side of her character, one had to meet her at work and, even then, in the bright moments of creative work. Then, Maria Tenisheva would irresistibly blaze forth with the sacred fire of creating, building, collecting, and preserving the treasures by which the spirit of man endures.

Indeed, she strove wholeheartedly and untiringly to safeguard the valuable shoots of art and knowledge. Every collector knows how zealously one should protect all constructive effort against the viselike grasp of those who aim to destroy it.

Let us sum up all that Maria Tenisheva has accomplished!

To the city of Smolensk, she gave a splendid museum, with many canvases that would arouse the envy of any metropolitan museum.

To the Russian museum, she donated a marvelous collection of watercolors, where side by side with the Russian painters were represented some of the best foreign masters. But the museum administration of that time did not comprehend the wide reach of such a gesture and refused to accept the foreign masterpieces. It appears as though we were unable to think beyond dead molds.

Let us remember another case of rank injustice. The diocese of Smolensk, with the benediction of its bishop, had placed and sold at auction sacred utensils from the Smolensk Cathedral sacristy. Maria Tenisheva, wishing to preserve these valuable artistic pieces for the city of Smolensk, commissioned the curator of her museum, Mr. Borstchevsky, to purchase them at the auction. But instead of gratitude for an action that benefitted the city of Smolensk, Maria Tenisheva was attacked in the papers by a certain General V. for "pillaging the Smolensk sacristy." The affair went to court and the slanderer was put to shame. But this goes to show the state of affairs in Russia at that time and the manner of attacks that the collector had to suffer in the interests of the people.

Many museums are indebted to Maria Tenisheva.

The Museum of the Society for the Encouragement of Fine Arts, the Museum of the Stieglitz School Society, the Museum of the Moscow Archaeological Institute, and many others contain donations from Maria Tenisheva.

Many schools were founded by her and others supported by her. And, finally, there was the art nucleus at

Talashkino where Maria Tenisheva tried to assemble the best men of art for the revival of artistic principles.

Let us remember the artistic workshops organized in Talashkino. Let us remember the inspiring plays. Let us remember the art students who were sent abroad to study, to that same studio where later Maria Tenisheva herself found refuge. Let us remember all the measures taken by Maria Tenisheva to increase the production of artistic handicraft and embroidery among the peasants of the Smolensk province. Let us remember Rodnik, the arts and crafts store in Moscow. Let us remember the exceptional care with which Maria Tenisheva surrounded painters. Let us remember the fairy-like "*teremki*"* of Maliutin. Let us remember the excavations in the Kremlin of Novgorod, which were made possible through the support of Maria Tenisheva. Let us remember the archaeologists Prachov, Borstchevsky, Ouspensky. . . . Let us remember the exhibitions organized by this remarkable woman to show the importance of Russian art. Let us remember the musicians and the writers, both Russian and foreign, who came to Talashkino. Stravinsky wrote a passage from his "Sacred Spring" upon the balustrade of one of Maliutin's *teremki*. Let us remember that it was Maria Tenisheva who again came to Diaghilev's aid and helped to organize the splendid magazine *Mir Iskustva* (*The World of Art*), which proved to be the domain of new conquests of art.

One must keep in mind that it was not an easy task at the end of the nineties of the last century to break the bonds of "academism" and enter the ranks of the new art. Such a deed was never crowned by official laurels. On the contrary, every movement in that direction brought forth an avalanche of enmity and slander. But Maria Tenisheva had no fear of it. Besides, indifference to calumny also proves to be one of the characteristics of selfless seeking for truth. There is no doubt that

---

* In ancient Russia, *terem* (or *teremok*) was the most secluded part of a house, where women lived in complete privacy.

a weaker spirit than that of Maria Tenisheva could have found many reasons to give up the fight and to justify a withdrawal. Tenisheva, instead, turned to new spheres of activity. During the last years spent by her in Talashkino, she was attracted by the thought of building a church. We decided to call this church "The Temple of the Spirit." The central place in it was to be occupied by the painting of the Mother of the World.

Our common work, which had bound us previously, was now more crystallized by our common thoughts about the temple. All ideas about the synthesis of iconographic presentations gave great joy to Maria Tenisheva. Many things were planned for the church in our intimate conversations.

The first tidings of the war reached us while we were at work in the church. The plans came to a stop and were never completed. But if the greater part of the temple's walls have remained unpainted, nevertheless, the fundamental thought of this undertaking was expressed, and this crowning bequest of Maria Tenisheva in Talashkino showed how true she remained to her original tendency to build and believe in the future and in new ideas.

Later years held new wanderings for Maria Tenisheva, a complete change of her outward life and a revaluation of many people. I am sorry that, here in the Himalayas, I haven't with me one of her last letters, which should be quoted fully whenever an attempt to characterize her is made. In this remarkable letter, she expresses the fullness of her understanding of contemporary events. Leaving aside her personal feelings, passing by national and other considerations, Maria Tenisheva, without the slightest bitterness, transports her thoughts into the future, speaking in still more unifying tones.

Having only her work table, a small studio, and a tiny villa in the environs of Paris (I used to call it "Small Talashkino"), Maria Tenisheva found herself again free in her thoughts. She took no time for the appraisal of men's characters but spoke of the future—the future that is knowledge. The problem of art's heritage, expressed in the traditions and ornaments of the Far East, not only had not faded in her eyes but had acquired an added brilliancy. Yet she did not become a theorist. No shocks could tear her away from life. She was working, filled as before with the desire to give people the joys of art.

Of the various kinds of art, Maria Tenisheva had chosen for herself the most difficult and the most monumental. Her enamels, founded upon the principles of the ancient, age-old industry, are spread widely throughout the world. Her symbolic birds, Syrin, her white cities, her flowery glazes, her images of recluses indicate clearly the direction of her thoughts and creative work. The *Firebird*—of the enchanted country of the future—captivated and lifted her above everyday life. Here lay the source of her inviolable buoyancy of spirit and devotion to knowledge.

The enamels of Maria Tenisheva in French museums and in various private collections will be a living memory to her remarkable life and her striving toward the Fire Flower—Creative Work.

At a time when great masses of people were in the tumult of contemporary questions, forgetting the future in the froth of current events, Maria Tenisheva was interested in the migration of peoples and Gothic heritage, and asked me to find, in the depths of Asia, the necessary data for her problems, repeating, "It is absolutely necessary to find it. These enamels and this flowery ornament must be confirmed."

Maria Tenisheva learned about our departure for Central Asia when she was lying sick in her Small Talashkino.

"Well, Father Nicholas," she greeted me at our last meeting, "it seems as though you have really decided to build a temple." Her face bore an austere expression, and she reminded one of an Old Believer as she lay in bed, covered with a shawl. As we were leaving Small Talashkino,

my wife said to me, "She is a true Martha Possadnitza.*
What strength, what austerity!"

I can imagine how glad Maria Tenisheva would have
been to learn now, after our expedition, that her conjecture
about the migration of peoples was entirely correct. And
her joy would have been boundless could she have seen
some of the ornaments, ascertained the analogy between
Tibetan antiquities and those of Scythia and of Alan, and
seen Tibetan swords and fibulae that remind one of the
so-called Gothic antiquities.

No one can say that Maria Tenisheva did not follow
the right way.

Let us cite the names of those who at one time or other
collaborated with her and whom she held in high esteem.
They were Vrubel, Nesterov, Repine, Serov, Levitan,
Diaghilev, Alexander Benois, Bakst, Maliutin, Golovine,
Somov, Bilibine, Naumov, Zioglinsky, Yakuntchikove,
Polenova, and also many others who had worked in
Talashkino and in the other studios and undertakings of
Maria Tenisheva.

These names represent a brilliant epoch in Russian art,
that epoch that brought Russia out of the narrow, national
understanding and created her well-deserved reputation
for her art, which it now holds. And Maria Tenisheva,
by choosing precisely this group of artists who pursued
daring and diverse ideals, showed thereby the correctness
of judgment.

Maria Tenisheva loved the old Russian church painting and valued it very highly.

At the time when Russian church painting was still
within the boundaries of the history of art and of iconographic investigations, Maria Tenisheva had already
grasped the future artistic significance of this particular

---

* Martha Possadnitza stood at the head of the people of Novgorod
when they were fighting Ivan III in the fifteenth century, and urged
them to unflinching resistance.

art. In her appreciation of the icons, as we now see, Maria Tenisheva had also followed the right road.

In promoting education and raising the level of the lower classes of Smolensk, Maria Tenisheva accomplished a timely work, for the necessity of it was indeed evident. The correctness of her actions in this direction is incontestable.

Today, a large street in the city of Smolensk bears the name of Tenishevskaya Street. Indeed, many were the people who had walked along Tenishevskaya Street to receive enlightenment and still more are bound to go seeking predestined cultural possibilities.

In enriching the museums with the best examples of creative ability, Maria Tenisheva wanted to point out the importance for future culture in furthering the understanding of art and the esteem for this type of creative work. One can always admire those who strive to lay the foundations of future life.

About what has already been accomplished, we speak briefly and lightly: Let us remember all the schools, workshops, museums, and the efforts to promote education. It can be expressed in a few words, yet think of all the labor, care, and obstacles that each of these undertakings contained.

In turning to a broad understanding of religious principles it can be stated that here, too, Maria Tenisheva possessed opinions devoid of prejudice or superstition, which were adequate to the demands of the near future.

Opinions, keen and to the point, can sometimes irritate small minds, but is not keenness of judgment an attribute of culture and civilization?

I look back on the work done by Maria Tenisheva with a feeling of joy. We must highly value people who are able to arouse in us such a feeling of joy. May it follow her into the regions where she has departed, this feeling of joy, from the realization that she had yearned for a beautiful future and that her place is among those who are laying the steps of the coming culture.

Maria Tenisheva was a great woman—a true Martha Possadnitza.

Many years ago, when making excavations in the province of Tver, we visited the grave of Martha Possadnitza and heard the innumerable legends in which the people enshroud the name of this remarkable woman of Novgorod.

And I can clearly visualize now how gratefully the people of Russia will remember the name of Maria Tenisheva.

Many legends will be woven in Tenishevskaya Street, and the name of Maria Tenisheva will be engraved among those of the true "constructors."

CANIMUS SURDIS—
"SINGING TO THE DEAF"

"WE sing to the deaf!" sorrowfully exclaimed the great Roman poet. Again an avalanche of news! And again, about the same!

Many publishing houses on the Continent have been suspended. Financial difficulties in scientific circles of the world. Useful publications discontinued. Museums temporarily closed. Some terrifying figures of the unemployed. During the last year many banks have failed. H. G. Wells, well-known for his foresight, urges the necessity of the construction of a new Noah's Ark for the salvation of culture and civilization. Endless depression! Endless distressful news in letters and newspapers. Everywhere the dark forces first of all attack cultural manifestations. It seems as if culture hinders the carrying on of their satanic plans to destroy the world.

May the position of the ten millions of unemployed improve! May joyful buying return! But these calls are like the foam of waves against the rocks. From foam perhaps some useful product can be made! Perhaps, but so far, the oceanic waves of disastrous news rise and thunder furiously against culture.

Even kindhearted citizens are beginning to whisper, "Is it the right time to think of culture?" "What good is civilization if we have nothing to eat?" Big strong men fight the gigantic waves threatening the crumbling culture. Only read the words of a well-known author written with his heart's blood: "Our personal position is indescribably hard. Still we fight with our last efforts, keeping up our trust and vigor and love toward sincere friends. The only advantage of our position is the complete absence of the fear of tomorrow because anyhow it cannot be worse than today. But we are exhausted and have become older by ten years. Yet to stand up under the burden of debts for eight years without the possibility of doing what is most important, one has to be made of steel and be oak-like in resistance. The end of the world is nearing!"

We answer this strong and glorious fighter, "On a crossroad the passersby were asked with what they were building the future age? One sneered. "With poison gas!" Another, serpentlike, hissed. "With submarines!" The third laughed. "By short-selling." The fourth: "With golf." The fifth: "With narcotics." The sixth: "*Après nous, le déluge!*" The seventh: "Through culture!"

Is it not a miracle that out of seven passersby, one still remembered culture? And not only remembered but was not even ashamed to pronounce this word that is so inconvenient for many. Who knows, perhaps through this one word, this passerby already brought upon himself persecutions.

But even then it sounds miraculous, that amid the turmoil on the crossroad, still this sacred, inspiring, calling conception was pronounced. My friend thinks that only one in a hundred passersby will pay respect to the very foundation of life, which created the epochs of renaissance—all joy, all prosperity, all daringness, and all achievements.

Verily, if this panacea were to be given without toil, not at the edge of the precipice, not on the cross, not while facing the cup of poison, it would not be that precious gem—the very foundation of life. If difficulties are blessed, then verily they are so in the name of culture, which embodies the Light, the Great Service, unwaveringness of achievement, all beauty, and all knowledge.

If obstacles contain in themselves potential possibilities, then suffering for the cause of culture will unfold the precious silver Lotus within one's heart—but not to lose the entrusted Stone and not to spill the Chalice. Infinity is boundless. Not abstractedness, but life itself! Nowadays the list of failures is longer than the list of successes because mankind has rejected culture. Humanity has violated culture by regarding it as a luxury. Nobody will admit that we are now going through normal times. Even bandits, racketeers selfishly understand the abnormality of conditions and apply ingeniously their ghastly tricks in order to make the best of this hour of darkness. But there are many young hearts that respond to Light. One must only realize how urgently we must turn to everything cultural, to everything ennobling the taste and all the strivings of life. Although conscious fighters for culture are few, yet the more thanks and honor are deserved by those who stand as guardians of the true treasures of mankind. As antennas, they sound over the whole world and receive and send calls for upliftment, refinement, and constructiveness.

I remember when, in Mongolia, the expedition miraculously escaped a most dangerous situation, and a gray-haired Buriat solemnly raised his hand and exclaimed, "Light conquers darkness!" This was not something abstract, not a dream! And the sagacious dweller of the desert understood the reality of the Great Light; he understood that finally darkness was doomed to destruction. Thus those who walk with Light will be victorious in the end, but the wavering ones will be precipitated into the abyss of darkness.

Is it possible that there are so many deaf people?

Sometimes it seems as if the path of culture and the conditions of life have separated. But if the levers of a machine lose coordination, then naturally one cannot expect full speed and one cannot avoid disastrous knocks.

Even the mind of a child understands that enlightenment, education, culture are as fuel to a motor.

The troglodyte threatens, "To hell with culture! Cash first." But because of this conception, he is called a troglodyte; and his place is in a cave, but not in the Hall of Culture.

The troglodyte finds even during a disaster enough

gold to buy himself a bloody spectacle of a bullfight or a cockfight or races, or to delight himself at the sight of the breaking of skulls or dislocation of limbs, or in carnal desires. For such entertainments money is always plentiful. There will even be found some hypocritical excuses in muttering something about physical health. But as soon as we approach the urgent questions of the ennoblement of taste, the questions of creativeness and ascension of the spirit, we find the ears and eyes closed. Thus one understands the origin of the old French proverb: "He is especially deaf who does not want to hear." The Italian poet who exclaimed, "We sing to the deaf!" also knew these deaf ones.

At the same time, one also reads news about a new bullet that pierces every armor, of new shields protecting the back in crawling attacks, of new deadly gases and similar "humanitarian" appliances.

On the same pages some voices rise in indignation against fratricide. But the troglodyte roars with triumphant laughter because he thinks that he succeeded in separating the levers of the machine. The saturnine Alberich and Mime hope that their rule is at hand, when everything connected with Light will be humiliated and Satan himself, without any trouble, will receive all that he desires.

The appearing of troglodytes is terrible.

Unfortunately, it is not exaggerated. Advertisements of evening gowns, festivals, dinners, and prizefights do not hide the misfortunes. Practically in every newspaper, one sees some news about the curtailing and discontinuation of cultural undertakings.

Thus the troglodytes triumph; they think that their doctrine of gluttony and lust is already coming to rule above everything. As if special internationals of light and darkness were being formed. No prize fanfares will deaden this Armageddon.

Is it not the last hour to unite everyone to whom culture is not an empty sound? Is it not the last hour to stop the suppression of everything valuable, creative, and young?

When you speak of gluttony, lust, speculation, then maybe your sincerity will not be questioned; but every attempt to turn to beauty, to knowledge, to the meaning of life will be followed by mistrust and suspicion of insincerity. Well, you may say that the proverb "*Homo homini lupus*"—"One man is a wolf to another"—dates not from yesterday, and that the moon and the sun are still the same.

It is true that long ago another poet exclaimed, "In eternal beauty shines indifferent nature," and "to good and evil, we are shamefully indifferent," but these lines about indifference referred to people who knew, it would seem, far less than the people of today.

At present even nature is not quite indifferent. Even in remote mountains, people speak of unusual earthquakes, of volcanic eruptions, of sunspots. And an institute in Nice comments, in almost astrological expressions, upon the influence of sunspots on human beings, if one is to believe the latest communications of *Le Matin.*

But the present persecution of culture is not due to sunspots. And dark spots of irresponsibility on the human conscience come by no means from the sun. These spots of irresponsibility are due to darkness, to ignorance.

"Ignorance is the greatest crime"—so it has been ordained by ancient commandments. He who dares to say, "To hell with culture!" is the greatest criminal. He is the seducer of the coming generation; he is the murderer; he is the sower of darkness; he is the suicide.

"We sing to the deaf!" sorrowfully exclaimed the poet of Rome. But the poet of "Beda, the Preacher" answered with cosmic vigor:

"Silent became the sage, drooping his head.
But before he had ceased, the Stones from all
    the world's ends
Thundered in answer: '*Amen!*'"

III

WHEN ARMAGEDDON ROARED

THOU SHALT NOT KILL

BEFORE me lies an imposing volume *The First World War.* The publishers of it no doubt desired to show all the negative moments of the war and its consequences. Such books are excellent indicators amid the search and appeals for peace. If we witnessed all these horrors in the age of civilization and great discoveries, it means that the world culture is greatly shaken.

Besides its text, that book horrifies the reader with its pictorial reproductions. Let us not enumerate all such disgraces of humanity. It is sufficient to look into the eyes of a starving child-skeleton in order to feel into what abyss savagery and bestiality lead. The shameful destructions of the majestic creations of human genius also appeal to the hearts that are not yet fossilized.

The meaning of this white book on a table is similar to our white Banner of Peace, which was discussed at the Washington Convention. The more such books, the more signs of a reminder, the more the human heart will shudder and will ponder about the closest measures for the protection of dignity, for the safeguarding of the noble seal of the age. For what can be more dishonorable for such a seal of the age than the destruction of culture in its deep significance?

We must be thankful to all those who, by one sign or another, try to decrease the field of killing and destruction. It is true, we are horrified looking at some of the pages of the book of the Great War, but we exclaim at the same time: Let the school teacher, when showing such books to the students, say, "This will not be repeated."

So much terror has entered life, destroying the moral and material bases, that indicators should undeferrably appear on perilous spots from which humanity must be saved!

But in order that the teacher should have the right not to conceal from the children past horrors, he must cover every page of horrors with ten volumes of the true heroic deeds of humanity. He must know how to speak beautifully about those who shed their blood for the defense of the best constructive and educational foundations. Therefore, every publisher who shows the horrors takes upon himself the duty to issue books depicting the best images of the heroes and leaders of mankind.

In the days of the world crises, the wise Commandments should be especially remembered. Among them the most outstanding and imperative is: Thou shalt not kill! During the millenniums of bygone ages, the spiritual leaders of mankind on all continents repeatedly and patiently reminded of this closest basis of life. Precisely, this commandment has in view the safeguarding of life—that greatest gift for self-perfectment. And again, this planetary command was sent out, but again the blacksmiths of the whole world untiringly forged swords and spears, presupposing attacks, slaughter, and murders.

Endless volumes have been written against the killing of the body. From all sides it has been shown to what an extent this cruel action does not correspond to human dignity. If one could collect all the sayings that have accumulated around this conception, then we would see an amazing wreath, and on every leaf of it would twinkle the tears of humanity of all ages and all nations.

But amid the confusion of life, it has become unbefitting and even shameful to speak about this Commandment. And he who dares will be regarded as an impotent pacifist of the most perverted kind. He who speaks of this Commandment will be considered, if not insane, then at least a suspicious character who upsets the social structure of contemporary conventionalities. Indeed, if in antiquity murders were counted by the thousands, then in our "enlightened, civilized" era, the number of killed exceeds many millions. If in the Stone Age, hunters with primitive bows and spears killed some animals, then now in the slaughterhouses of Chicago alone, within the shortest time, some fifty thousand animals' lives have been taken. Such is progress!

And if with all the scientific data at hand, you will try to advocate the advantage of the nutritive value of a vegetarian diet, you will again be suspected of some intentions directed against society. Civilized humanity, often reiterating the word "culture," still regards blood as something highly nutritive; and there still exist ignorant physicians who prescribe raw, bloody meat. Lamentable dicta—whatever you will say about blood, meat, about the cruel pastime of hunting, or about the so-much-liked-by-the-mob executions, all this will be permitted as a befitting conversation in the parlor rooms of highest society. As they taste a sugar-coated biscuit and dip their lips in the famous cup of tea, you can smilingly relate how during a certain execution, not only was all available space filled with excited onlookers, but even from all windows and roofs of adjoining houses, people were staring at such a "rare" sight. If you will narrate without much criticism, then the society will enrich such themes with many piquant details.

Thus, together with the amount of ordainments against killing, there also grows the very number of murders of both animals and human beings. Many wiseacres will state: "Such is the law of life." And if you will contradict, quoting authoritative Commandments, then your interlocutor will reply, "You are yet too young," as if, according to his opinion, old age is the symbol for bloodthirstiness and cruelty.

Cruel are the deeds of this world. On the one side, people try to discover all sorts of remedies to prolong life; and on the other, they, with still greater speed, invent deadly guns and poisonous gases, which, besides destroying human life, poison the whole planet and inflict much greater harm than the civilized modern consciousness wishes to admit. All this refers to the body. But let us not forget that besides the body, we should keep in mind the human spirit, consciousness, thought, and ideas that govern the world. Of this a multitude of philosophers of all ages wrote and spoke, and in confirmation of this truth, they went into the fire and onto the scaffold.

But now the enmity of the world has reached such a state, that to speak of the perversion or violation of the spirit is considered merely a bigotry of bad manners. And indeed, where now can people hear about vital ethics, about the purification of consciousness, and the discipline of thought? The churches insufficiently stress it, and we all remember how guns were brought for blessing into churches. In schools there is no chair of ethics, and yet this subject, in all its historical vividness, could be one of the most inspiring. The ethics of the spirit, the teaching of the heart, has behind itself a most beautiful literature in all epochs. But it is not the custom to read such fundamental chronicles. It is not in the habit to search in characteristic old expressions something needed even today. For us who are addicted to aimless speeding to bodily contests, can there be any time to inspire ourselves with the beauty of ancient conceptions and images?

Having transplanted our consciousness into bazaars, into stock exchanges, into stadiums, into every possible kind of race and super-race, we simply lose the understanding wherein lies that self-perfectment for which we are here on this earth. One may run faster than his neighbor. One may fly faster than birds, but one may also swallow up one's neighbor more bloodthirstily than a tiger. Embitterment has generated that unheard-of negation that destroys the meaning of human achievement. We had an opportunity once to quote the most significant statement of a British engineer-inventor, who said that humanity is not ready to accept great discoveries. And H. G. Wells, not because of the triumph of culture, recently suggested building a new Noah's Ark.

Verily, in home life, in the schools, in social activities,

many lessons of cruelty are taught. And in exchange, how blankly and tiresomely is repeated the withered command: Thou shalt not kill! And in the physical body, people have ceased to understand what it means, not to kill; what higher meaning this commandment, austere in its brevity, has.

And when matters reach the stage of killing the spirit, the murdering of the consciousness and of the heart, then our contemporary dictionary comes into complete disorder and turns out to be altogether useless. But the threatening crisis of the world, we repeat, is not in the bazaar, but in our hearts. Until people understand the meaning of pre-ordained self-perfectment, they will not be in a position to value the whole practicability of the command not to kill not only the body but also the spirit.

Some dark instigators shout, "To hell with culture!" "To hell with heroes, leaders and teachers!" But precisely through these renovated conceptions can construction and betterment enter life.

Embitterment, after all, leads to poverty, to perpetual dissatisfaction, in which even wealth appears as poverty. Cruelty makes of the heart that stone that we try to throw at our neighbor, instead of illumining the near ones with the light of cooperation. In the conception of cooperation, no thought of killing will enter because cooperation needs life and not death. In the difficult days I want to greet friends with this blissful cooperation, which will bring us to a mutual understanding of the high meaning of self-perfectment.

Always when we pronounce the great commandment: "Thou shalt not kill," let us understand it not only in its physical but mainly in its spiritual sense. This last meaning will direct our attention to the heart and will help us understand the great Commandment not only in the narrow earthly way but in the whole magnificence of all higher worlds.

Cooperation, cognizance, strengthening of the spirit

will again give to the world those heroes that the hearts of mankind long for.

Friends, do not think that these lines were written now, after the Second World War. No, they were written after the First World War, and now the same alarm should be sounded by all megaphones, by all loudspeakers, but in a superlative way. It is a shame that such superlatives should resound, that humanity should again be exhorted to ponder over the terrible reminiscences and truisms. Mankind knows that nothing humanitarian has been learned during this quarter of a century. Utilitarianism has led to atomic bombs. German militarism has resulted in unheard of bestialities. Will we again exclaim with Leonardo da Vinci, *"Pazzia bestialissima!"*

SELF-SACRIFICE OF EVIL

EVERY step of constructive good also calls forth the special attention of the dark forces. We have often noticed that the dark forces turn out to be, in daily life, even better organized than the forces striving toward Light—this is very deplorable. At the time when those who consider themselves servitors of the Good shamefully permit themselves every kind of destructive disunion, the spiteful entities act very unitedly and are well organized. This is a very sad spectacle, yet one may observe this rather often, beginning from small everyday questions up to affairs of state. And the energy that is being developed by the dark forces sometimes even leads them to a peculiar form of self-sacrifice.

No doubt everyone can recall a great many instances when an evildoer, a slanderer, a traitor began to act even to his own disadvantage, and yet in the name of enacted evil, already he could no longer stop himself. He was ready to put his reputation at stake; he was ready to challenge the powerful enemy; he was ready to face ridicule—only to continue the evil sowing that he had once commenced.

The psychological reasons of such an apparently abnormal manifestation as the self-sacrifice of evil are difficult to formulate. Of course, first of all they have their root in the limitation of evil. Evil, after all, is always ignorant in something or other and can never reach a high state of consciousness. The methods of evil are, in the majority of cases, rather primitive, and sooner or later this circumstance must come to light, which is, by no means, a self-consolation for those who have been subjected to the attacks of evil. It will be but the confirmation of the immutable law of limitation and thus of the impracticability of evil. But if one can speak of a self-sacrifice of evil, which even risks its own destruction in order to commit a crime or some evil, then how much better should the forces of good be organized in order not to bemean their neighbor and brother warrior! It would seem that all fellow travelers should already be considered desirable friends. People very easily pronounce such words as "friendship, "amity," and "cooperation." But all this, in its very essence, is very easily subjected to the influence of evil. By way of self-consolation, it is said that this is not the fault of the seekers for good but that of the zealous soldiers of evil, who, as if by their resourcefulness and with much ingenuity, sever the knot of cooperation. And when giving such praises to evil, people do not realize at all what a disgrace they attribute to the potentiality of Good. For the acknowledgment of the power of evil is already the best praise.

Verily, the acknowledgment of the power and ingenuity of evil already in itself contains the potentiality of disintegration and the bemeaning of Good. Instead of trying in a fit of fear and cowardice to vindicate oneself through the power of evil, would it not be better to think how easily and naturally all good strivings may be applied for self-defense?

And the problem is not only in the self-defense of good. Every good is already in itself active and fills the immeasurable, far-off space. If evil strikes and infests the atmosphere, then Good is a true healer and renewer of injured tissues.

It would also seem quite natural that constructive Good should be especially sharpened and vigilant in the moments of the so-called Armageddon—at the hour of attack of the dark forces. Yet we see that at this hour, which is so great because of its consequences, the good forces are becoming permeated with unbefitting timidity, leaving the field of action to the forces of darkness.

It is sad to see how not only the forces of darkness themselves but also their greyish allies lie and slander and sow weeds without any resistance from the side of those who yet consider themselves the guardians of Truth and Good. It is deplorable to see how these deserters into the camp of darkness, without even pondering over the consequences, join malicious sowers. It is strange that, at that moment, their feelings of responsibility for the committed evil become completely atrophied. In their repulsive convulsions, these volunteers of evil do not even care for their position or rank or age but only for the sowing of their destructive seeds. It is incomprehensible that the experience of age, not to speak of the responsibility of education, does not stop the liars and slanderers. And the voluntary allies of evil shamelessly continue to call themselves among the ranks of esteemed and honored men.

Besides, the liar will not even go to the trouble of checking his cunning devices on facts, but on the contrary, will, by every conceivable way, hasten to evade such possibilities. Whenever confronted with facts, he even falls into a state of physical convulsions and trembles when seeing that his malicious machinations are in danger of becoming disclosed. Perhaps sometimes the liar himself does not believe in his innermost, in his own slander, its obvious untruthfulness, but some inexpressible process compels him to slide down the incline. And then his formulas of definition become especially rich, and before them the timid of the defenders of Truth often become pale. And are there many who can find the daringness to say at least, "Do not speak of what you do not know?" For if to someone the measure of good is not clear, then at least the clean, sound adherence to facts should be the primitive condition of the human standard.

It is also regrettable to observe another variety of the volunteers of evil, who often do not even support a lie in words but who silently rejoice. They do not even try to warn the slanderer of the consequences of his lie: On the contrary, by their quiet smiles they encourage the doers of evil. Thus, between the conscious forces of darkness and warriors of active Good, there is a legion of volunteers of evil, who, in most varying degrees, assist and hiddenly back the infection of the atmosphere.

The discipline of spirit, the inherent consciousness of responsibility, which is inseparable from human existence, does not worry these malicious evildoers. One can give them no other name, for they go without a path and in their ignorant licentiousness are ready to join any destructive infection.

All these qualities are neither national nor are they subject to other divisions. These considerations are purely all-human and prove once more that the forgotten living ethics are necessary, first of all, beginning from the first days of education.

Pondering over the self-sacrifice of the forces of darkness, symptoms of which people see so often, they should, sooner or later, also think of the practicability of the same active self-sacrifice on the part of Good. The examples of wonderful heroes are, it would seem, sufficiently real. It would also seem that not for abstract and hazy, unreal problems but for a true constructiveness, these great souls labored here on our earth, affirming their thoughts and words by daily incessant actions. The vocabulary of the self-sacrifice of Good is indeed beautiful and by far more complete than the casual and conventional encyclopedia had yet time to record. Becoming saturated with these telling examples, people, and mainly the younger generation, can so easily turn away from the unconscious support of evil or even of the closest cooperation in malicious destruction. It is an old-known truth that children in their first years usually respond easily to Good.

It is also usually so that the sad examples of the family awaken in the child's soul for the first time a leaning toward evil and thereafter of active participation in it. But now, if in the whole world the tension reaches its climax, if even the cosmic forces respond to these destructive infections, then it is indeed high time to become ashamed for the activity of evil that has reached a stage of self-sacrifice. For the very definition of the self-sacrifice of evil should awaken in even very ignorant people the desire for similar action in the name of constructive Good.

The self-sacrifice of evil is indeed a serious reproach to humanity! After the terrific effects of the atomic bombs, it became very fashionable to declare that atomic energy will be used solely for beneficial purposes. Let it be so! Nevertheless, in the memory of mankind forever will remain a shameful reminiscence that the highest energy was first brought to the Earth for destruction.

Everybody is fully aware that billions of dollars will never be spent for educational and beneficial purposes. But will it not turn, once again, into the self-sacrifice of evil?—Jinns helping to construct temples?

Maynard Shipley in his *Principles of Electricity,* says: "Several eminent physicists are now specializing on the problem of how to liberate and control intra-atomic energy for man's uses—or abuses.

"Bearing in mind the present intellectual, moral and economic status of our 'leaders of thought' and remembering that one pound of common soil contains intra-atomic energy equal to the destructive power of more than a million tons of dynamite, let us hope that the secret of releasing and 'controlling' intra-atomic energy will not be discovered in our day and age."

Indeed, let us hope that out of the greatest evil will come the highest Good.

BENEVOLENCE

WHEN one remembers Bhagawan Sri Ramakrishna, Swami Vivekananda, and all the leaders of the Ramakrishna Mission and its centers, there always comes to mind the concept of benevolence. Benevolence is a powerful word. Both of its constituent parts presuppose an accumulation of blissful force. *Bene* means the Good in its entire constructive sense. *Volence*—volition—is the power of thought and will. And when this immense high might is directed toward the upliftment of humanity, it represents the true essence of the Sri Ramakrishna movement. In this movement there is revealed so much of a direct self-sacrificing labor. Precisely, there is a constant benefaction, untiringly and gloriously penetrating into the hearts.

All these good words are easily pronounced, but for the ordinary person, it is not easy to manifest them in life. The very thought, the art of thinking, requires education and training. And only in the process of doing good does benevolence receive its vital significance. In the same good-doing is created a better future. This is not a truism; on the contrary, at present all nations should exercise the art of thinking in this direction. Let us beware that somewhere, instead of benefaction, there should not appear the ugly grimace of malefaction.

People sometimes think about the future, yet very often it does not enter at all into vital deliberations. Indeed, it is not entirely within human forces to determine the future, but each one should strive for it with all of his consciousness. And not to a beclouded future should one aspire but to precisely a better future. In this striving will already be the pledge of success.

On days of solemnity, prayer is uplifted about the future. No misty abstractions does it affirm. In it are expressed three principles—realization of that which is most lofty, the building of world peace, and benevolence—as the fundamentals of existence. Without these three bases, construction is impossible; yet they must not be promised abstractly but in their full and undeferrable reality. It would seem that the third-mentioned principle ought to be the most ordinary feature of everyday life. Only benevolence! Only goodwill and altruism! For whom? Why, for people themselves. For those with whom the task has been set to pass over this field of life.

It is a fact that no deep studies and instructions are needed for benevolence. It would seem that it is already presupposed at each human encounter. Can it be possible to draw near to any human being without fundamental goodwill? How is it possible to meet a neighbor with hatred or suspicion, or even with plotted villainy? Where then, in what sort of covenants, written or unwritten, have malice and suspicion been ordained?

"Man is a wolf to man." Surely this is one of the most malignant aphorisms. For so much results from auto-suggestion. If one hears from the cradle about good, then it, too, will surely remain a guiding principle. Even all the confusions of corrupted life will not eradicate the concept of good. Where man has been accustomed to live in good, there he values all the remarkable significance of the word "benevolence." Surely this word is very imperative. Volition, formulated will . . . This is already something accomplished, done!

Volition cannot only be instinctive. It is promoted in full consciousness, in full responsibility. Perhaps each state council ought to be opened with the important question: "Is there benevolence?" And he who remains silent should take no part. It will probably be said that precisely the malicious ones will themselves cry out about benevolence. And here, too, an imprint of human radiations would show the truth.

Heart radiations would show the true feelings, without the mask of insincerity. How mottled would be the radiations of the false, the insincere! The man who has not pondered upon the deep significance of benevolence will not often understand in general what is being spoken about here! Why underline words known to all and which, moreover, have never improved anything? Of course such monstrous opinions are possible.

Not seldom a vendor cries out something very useful, absolutely without thinking about the meaning of the words uttered by him. Does a scribe often know the contents of what he has copied? Sometimes even one who reads aloud to another thus frees himself, as it were, from an understanding of what he reads. In such a manner often the most valuable and urgent considerations become meaningless words.

Is a better future possible without benevolence, without benevolence in all its solemnly imperative meaning? What sort of peace will there be on earth without benevolence? And where will be the "glory in the highest" without a profound and unceasing desire for good?

A better future. You must be better today than yesterday. If there is no longing for this, then surely from that which is most important and already ordained, only a negligible fraction will remain. All the great signs may be in readiness. But if there be no desire for the sake of good to follow them, then what part of them will be perceptibly carried out? Who then has the right to vitiate or belittle that which has been composed by great paths? Surely this is no empty dreaming but the responsibility of the messenger.

Even a simple postman in twilight and in darkness proceeds with caution in order not to stumble, in order that a branch may not lash him in the eye, in order to avoid wild beasts. Yet he bears someone else's letter about which he knows nothing. When, then, man thinks about the future, when he takes into consideration all its conditions and all good wishes, how much more strivingly and carefully does he proceed, ready and alert. He proceeds vigilant and imbued with feeling. He makes haste in order not to pilfer an ordained hour, and in his heart sounds glory in the Highest, and peace on earth, and benevolence for his neighbor.

Benevolence needs to be taught. Peace needs to be established. With every palpitation of the heart, one should be enraptured by glory in the Highest!

Examples of the creation of a better future may be drawn from various domains. One of them has remained in memory from early school years.

We were all tremendously impressed by the story of Schliemann—the noted investigator of Troy. We were all entranced by how he, from early years, set himself to the task of future researches, and how he began to prepare himself in all the branches of learning, and how he tenaciously enriched himself with knowledge and yet, at the same time and just as perseveringly, amassed a fortune. Of course, he maturely thought out all the resources he would need.

After many years of conscious labor, he brought to science his precious offering and remained the forefather of many brilliant investigators coming after him. One can imagine how, in his time, the businessmen shrugged their shoulders at the scholarly tasks of Schliemann. Likewise, one can see how other scholars, probably more than once, labeled him as an amateur and made fun of his undertakings. Yet with originality and persistence, he composed his own scientific future.

That which for another would have been attainment was for Schliemann only a means that had an applied relative value. In so many years of conscious labor is a large share of selflessness.

One can find in the history of the world many examples of such self-sacrificing attainments. But why dig in ancient annals when in our age we have the glorious examples of the lives of Bhagawan Sri Ramakrishna and Swami Vivekananda? In them is manifested the highest blissful benefaction and a leonine striving into a better future. And in what simple, all-penetrating words were expressed their outlines of spiritual unfoldment? May everyone be blessed who can speak of the Good in simple words. All the heaps of evil thoughts have deviated humanity from simplicity and constructive work. Every day, people are accustomed to witnessing destruction and murder. It is shocking with what indifference people imbue the abhorrent stories, which altogether do not befit humanity. With every day these horrors and cruelheartedness grow. Every place where the word "benevolence" is affirmed becomes a true shrine and stronghold of a better future.

Thus, let us again recall the beautiful word "benevolence." Verily, the conscious creators of a better future are filled with true benevolence.

HOMUNCULUS

I KNOW thee, O homunculus!* It is thou who didst supply us with so many unnecessary things on our journey. It was thou who didst advise us to distrust all that was young and "inexperienced." It was thou who didst put external facts in the place of the facts of spirit and of essentiality. It was thou who didst gild the frames of the pictures. Thou hast penetrated into councils and leagues and hast hidden the search for perfection with the duties of the grave-digger. Thou art working hard. And within thine unseen kingdom flourishes a most noble hatred of mankind.

Yet, for all that thou art small, we have observed thee already. And we have learned thy ways. Thou fearest the talisman of love. And love cuts the ground from under what thou buildest. The love of creative perfection! Harmony!

Thou dreamest of burying it under worn-out things. Thou thinkest that the flame of love will flicker out. But thou hast forgotten the mysterious property of the flame! It will light any number of torches, and never will it grow any less.

How then canst thou fight? And even shouldst thou penetrate into all the Leagues of the Nations, forget not that behind the nations stands humanity. And here industrious homunculus will not attain success. For, after all, humanity, however slowly, is progressing toward harmony.

Does it not seem strange to you, my friends, that even in our days, these days of extreme turmoil and terror, it is, nevertheless, possible to show forth actively such still

---

* The symbol of human vulgarity.

far-off conceptions as love, goodness, perfection, that is, all the companions of harmony. Harmony is often misunderstood. Harmony is not an abstract chanting of hymns. Harmony, the harmonization of the centers, is the manifestation of activity in all its might, in all its clarity and convincingness. Apprehending what we want, we combine all of our centers into one effort and even overcome all the ordinances of destiny. And our spirit knows, better than any, where truth lies. And every one of our actions is judged by the spirit of truth.

And it is this spirit that knows also that love and perfection will be applied in life in the simplicity and clarity of creative work. If the simplicity of expression, the clearness of desire correspond to the immeasurable majesty of the Cosmos, then the path will be a true one.

And this Cosmos is not the unattainable one, before which professors can only knit their brows, but that great and simple one that penetrates the whole of our life, building up mountains and setting light to stars on all the countless planes of the Universe.

Simplicity is an inevitable quality of harmony. The creative work of the future will be imbued with simplicity. You will not, of course, confuse simplicity with primitiveness, with assumption. The difference here is as great as between a work of art and a print. And often in gilded frames, we find mere commercial prints, while true art is fluttering on a poster in the wind and snow.

But the spirit, even in silence, knows which is the print, the banal, and which is joy and creative work.

Silently question your spirit as you bring every object into your house. Repeating incantations against the homunculus, think why and how you have arrived at the idea of bringing a new guest to your hearth.

Remember that these silent guests may become true friends, but may also become enemies to your home.

In the cognizance of objects lies their harmony. And again your spirit distinguishes friend from foe.

We know the immutable healing of music and color.

Let us recall the power of song. Let us recall the exaltation experienced in temples, in museums. The House of the Great Mystery. Art alone can clothe the Great Mystery with flesh. And the sacrament of the Spirit has only beauty for its base.

Of course you love art. And you would ask me many things: You want to know what is best for the harmony of the house—easel painting or photographs? Is it better to fix the surroundings once for all? Or is there more vitality in the idea, obtained from China and Japan, where every day one new picture is hung upon the wall of a room? No doubt you would ask as to the correctness of the idea of our modern exhibitions, where behind the appearance of the temple of art lurks the booth of the shopkeeper.

The Master drove the money changers out of the Temple. The Master knew, of course, that, as yet, we cannot do without them in our daily life, but it was out of the Temple that he drove them. So is it in the matter of art. Buying and selling, of course, must as yet remain. But they must be expelled from the Temple. Let the feast be open; let the shop be open too. But the shop in the Temple and the likeness of the Temple in the shop create internal corruption in those who create, and cynicism among those who look on. The sweet savor of the Temple will arrest the gesture even of the barefaced cynic, and the homunculus must flee. Verily, O homunculus, you will have to desert our life after all. Countless youthful hearts request you to depart.

Having purified the principle of remuneration of art, it becomes possible to introduce the latter into the home, to bring into it, as it were, a taper lit in the Temple. Both the idea of wall paintings and the precious change of impressions, as in the East, will find a place in it. For the truth is infinite. And every individual case of the affirmation of art is determined by the consciousness of the spirit.

The railway guard assumes that people do nothing but travel. In the mind of the shoemaker, men do nothing but walk. In the conception of the man of today, people do nothing but suffer. But in the knowledge of the Blessed, men must rejoice.

True, just at this moment, joy over art often sounds strange. Much is said about art, and yet so little art is brought into men's lives. And always excellent excuses and explanations are offered for this. It is always the most convincing circumstances that are to blame. Everything is to blame attaches only to the "civilized" man who goes to see bullfights or to watch fisticuffs carried on according to the rules of the ring. Here, both hearts and purses are open.

Question these people as to how much they have done for art. How much art have they brought into their lives? They will only be surprised at the question, and you will find that the caveman of the Stone Age holds the advantage over these conquerors of the earth. Nowadays, one has to speak of this too.

How is one not to speak of it when at the present time there are governments that seek to burden the freedom of art with special taxes and thereby put fresh obstacles in the thorny path of beauty. Here again is the work of the homunculus!

And at the same time, only ten in a hundred among the people bring art into their daily lives and know something about it. About 20 percent only talk about art without making any application of it. The remaining 70 percent, generally speaking, do not know, or rather, do not now remember what art is.

But it is better to reiterate, even if mechanically, "good, good, good," than to repeat, even though it be with a grin, "evil, evil, evil." This relative principle has been accepted by many. So in this way, let us ask ourselves, if only once a week, what have we done for art during the past seven days? Let politicians, too, and congressmen, clergymen, bankers, and businessmen, and all those who pride themselves on their often Sisyphean labors—let them, too, learn this very easy habit. Where men cannot follow the path of the joy of consciousness, let the pavement of this road be laid. But efforts are necessary; otherwise, our day threatens the work of art with special calamities. Art must flourish and the spiritual call of music must ring out independent of the state of the stock exchange and of the meetings of the League of Nations.

One more "non-platitude." Let us confess and remember that which is verily needful to remember. In the education of children, we still forget the development of the creative power. First, men seek to instill into the child a mass of conventional concepts. First, he is taken through a full course of fear. Then the child is acquainted with all the family quarrels. Then he is shown films, those criminal films in which evil is so inventive and brilliant, and good so dull and ungifted. Then the child is given teachers who, unfortunately, being often without any love for their subject, reiterate the deadening letter thereof. Further, the children are shown all the vulgar headlines in the daily press. Next, the child is plunged into the sphere of so-called "sport" that its young head may grow accustomed to blows and broken limbs. And this is how the youth's time is first occupied; he is given the most ignoble and perverted formulae. And after that, besmirched and rusted, he may begin creative work.

This is one of the deepest of crimes. Any machine, men treat with greater care than they treat a child. Of course—the machine has been paid for with "almighty" money. It may be allowed to grow dusty or be soiled with dirt. But no money is paid for the children.

We are often astonished by the unexpected character of a child's drawing, by the melody of a child's song, or by the wisdom of a child's reasoning. Where everything is yet open, there things are always beautiful. But afterward we notice that the child ceases to sing, ceases to draw, and that his reasoning begins to remind one of so-called children's books. The infection of triviality has already sunk into him, and all the symptoms of this horrible disease have become evident. Ennui has made its appearance, a conventional smile, submission to what is disagreeable, and finally, the fear of loneliness. Something near, some ever-present, guiding principle has therefore withdrawn, receded.

But you will not drive the children out of the Temple. Are not the most difficult things so very simple?

But if even a machine suffers from dust and dirt, how destructively must spiritual crime be to the tender young soul. In mortal yearning the little head seeks for light. Immortal pain it feels for all the offensiveness of its surroundings. It suffers, weakens, and sometimes lies in the dust forever. And the creative apparatus runs down and all its wires fall away.

Open in all schools the path to creative effort, to the greatness of art. Replace banality and despondency by joy and seership. Preserve the child from the grimace of life. Give him a bold, happy life, full of activity and bright attainments.

Develop the creative instinct from the earliest years of childhood.

Those scourges of humanity—triviality, loneliness, and weariness of life—will thus pass by the young soul of him who creates.

Open up the path of blessing.

Armageddon is roaring!

THE ISLAND OF TEARS

FOURTEEN years ago, I wrote in my diary:
Perhaps the most difficult necessity is the necessity of refusal—refusal to those who come to you with the best possible motives and decisions, who seek help for some excellent purpose that already exists, and that you are entirely without power to help. And not only that you cannot help, but scanning the entire horizon, you do not even know where to direct those who are in need so that their beautiful wants can be satisfied. A collection of all the messages asking for help becomes the true island of tears.

Sometimes you still can assume that some of these people will hold out until new conditions arise; but not seldom do you feel that their call is the last call, and that there is not only no reserve of further physical means, but that already the spiritual means are exhausted—and this is the saddest thing. Besides many personal misfortunes, it is terrible to see that all sorts of educational and cultural institutions are being uprooted. Mankind must be especially cautious of that which occurs precisely at this present time—the cutting down of the growth of culture, a culture, which by its blossoming, must bring a true prosperity, a spiritual prosperity, and prosperity in every form.

Here before us lies a request concerning a school. If it is not answered, many little children will remain without a necessary education. Here, also, is attached a photograph of a great number of children in this group, and what nice, dear faces, notwithstanding their clothing! How healthy an element is felt in these little bodies that are ready for spiritual food! And the money asked for this school is not at all large, but there is no source from which to obtain it.

Here is a request for support from a magazine and a very useful publishing house. Everything issued by this publishing house is valuable and absolutely useful. This is not some visionary dream. On the table are lying their most useful books, which transmit to the new generations beautiful, basic, and strengthening facts. Precisely, such magazines and publishing houses, fully constructive, must not only exist but also broaden, in the name of underlying necessity, toward perfection. And again the requested sum is so small, so small compared with the useful, already manifested achievements of the publishing house. Nevertheless, this sum is also missing. And again one has to write: "Let us await better times." These better times will come, but, until then, the whole tempo of already organized work will be disrupted. It is very probable that the work will soon cease, and you know what it means to reorganize the work anew. So many requests come from publishing houses and magazines, and they come not from one country, and they are not the result of the unhappiness of one people. The variety of nations, places, and all conditions converge in one focus, namely the focus of the fact that the sprouts of culture are curtailed.

Here before us is a completed and meritorious historical institution. The results of its fruitful publishing house and its publications are at hand. The list of coworkers contains in itself a whole number of the most valuable scientific names. The need of such an institution no one questions. The local government supported it as much as it could. But for its existence is still needed a sum, again ridiculous in its smallness, compared to the program of the institution. But even this sum is lacking. And how many valuable efforts, how much priceless time is being taken from the most necessary scientific researches for a fruitless search in order that the doors of the institution should not be closed altogether? And when they close, where will we go to find the necessary complex of strength and conditions? Is it possible that the spirit of mankind has become so profligate as to blindly throw away the most beautiful accumulations and the most necessary researches?

Also in the same position is a medical and scientific institution, which has already shown definite results and has been hailed by scientific centers; and here, also, is needed a ridiculously small sum, but it is not available. Just like the blade of the guillotine! Here, a very ancient museum, a national pride, is forced to seek the smallest sums in order to maintain itself. And again, the very same blade of the guillotine. Here are requests about the building of a Temple—so needed when the human spirit is sick. And instead of construction, the blade of the guillotine!

Here are the groups of youths who gathered in the name of beautiful, constructive beginnings, in the highest names and understanding—the most valuable centers of working youth, which struggle against their own straitened existence. And no matter how these seekers of the best spiritual strongholds search, they cannot find even a minimum sum in order to strengthen the existence of their unity. Weakened, they will scatter, driven by want. And when will one be able to unite them again—such valuable ones, who so rejoice in the spirit and in the heart.

Here is a cultural society, which is striving toward the tasks of education, culture, motherhood; toward the strengthening of all those principles, which if unrealized and unconstructed will cause us again to suffer a spiritual crash as well as a material one.

They are asking so little in order to exist! They give, as it is, everything that belongs to them that can be given. But these most beautiful examples of self-sacrifice are being broken before those icy currents about which the "Transmuting Fire" speaks.

And a well-known author, who was broadly hailed, cannot even write because he has no means for livelihood. Does not this express humanity's mad dissipation of its spiritual forces? And not only do all those manifold requests for the support of beautiful foundations remain unanswered because of want, but the universal order of things continues to tread the same destructive directions of sundering the best cultural projects and aspirations of mankind. And the serious thing is that this pertains not only to one country or even to one group of countries—no, this unwelcome news unquestionably comes from all parts of the world. Someone will say, "But schools continue to exist, universities continue to exist, and museums also exist." Yes, but let us see what the budgets of these institutions have gradually been reduced to, institutions that are being preserved only for the sake of longevity.

We read daily about the closing of entire scientific departments of museums: about the ceasing of research work, about the ceasing of excavations, about the stopping of construction, about the diminishing of the staffs through which so many needed, irreplaceable, young forces are being cut away in order to be lost forever in the ruthless ocean of chaos. "No" and "impossible" prevail. Denials and abolishments rule, even without special discussions, which are most necessary. Even in the endowed institutions, we see unprecedented notices about unfulfilled editions, about the delaying of plans, and again about the curtailing even of the most essential.

Of course, we must think about the future—of that not one will have another opinion. Even a manufacturer does not produce for yesterday. And now, amid the same existing ideas about the future, it would seem that people themselves, in the most cruel way, will begin to cut away everything, even that which is fundamentally necessary for every production.

The world has experienced many crashes and shocks. But is there not some sign of the spiritual and material misfortune that has now fallen upon mankind? Such a sign exists. And this sign will be terrible if special attention is not paid to it. This is the sign of universal misfortune. Heretofore, misfortunes were national or local, but now has come an unprecedented internationalism of misfortune. There is not one country, there is not one distant island that does not repeat its tales of misfortune.

The more in contact you come with the most varied peoples, the more shocked you are by the universality of misfortune. The small groups of those who lived on incomes that veiled the world with an illusory guaranty have become absolutely insignificant. Any of those who do not suffer as yet already speak about misfortune. And through these misfortunes, carrying affirmations and actions, come forth some destructive invocations of misfortunes, as if some invisible sowers of misfortune were passing through all the countries and throwing into space destructive, deadly formulas.

And following them appears a veritable dance of death: "Cut down, arrest, kill, deaden"—these deadly words, in many languages and in various formulas, are being carried all over the world. The phantom of economy has given birth to an army of the unemployed and has brought wages to a standard that does not answer even the most beggarly needs. Before us are figures of various wages, and one must confess that these figures are terrible.

One thing is clear: If mankind continues to hypnotize itself by invoking misfortune, it will violate that which is most valuable for its very existence: it will disrupt culture; it will disrupt the progress and accumulation of that which under different conditions is irrevocable or demands many centuries for curing.

The horror of refusal, the horror of killing living sprouts can no longer continue. It is absolutely necessary to cast aside personal quarrels and personal rivalry, and to think unitedly about the future generations, for whom the foundation of culture is the only stronghold of the spirit. Instead of calling forth misfortunes, sooner or later—and better it should be sooner—it is necessary to turn to the invocation of the foundation of positive construction; thus, we will begin to solve many so-called insoluble problems. Edison lived long; Michelson also lived long; and none of these creators of thought contemplated suicide. Creative thought is that accumulator of high energies that feeds all saps of life. The high energies of creativeness constitute the great elixir of life eternally sought by men. And this elixir of life proclaims to each one who desires to think, that it is necessary to turn from the destructive invocation of misfortune to the insistent call of benevolent, cultural constructiveness. And if we, all together, will call for the necessity of the development of knowledge and ennoblement, this call will, in itself, be the first stone in the new construction of the positive stronghold of mankind.

During the past fourteen years, terrible calamities have occurred, but today the same sorrowful lines can be repeated.

Our Lady of Culture! When shalt Thou descend upon our strife-torn earth?

IV

ON TO THE SUMMITS

THE ASCENT

ON ancient finger rings can be seen two spirals, one of ascent and one of descent. It is said that even a very lofty spirit can descend just as rapidly as it can ascend. This forewarning is very severe and just.

People have long understood that both ascent and descent can be extremely rapid. Nothing keeps even lofty beings from descent if they allow themselves to admit the baser desires. This path or rather leap into the abyss has more than once been dealt with both in Eastern and Western literature from the most ancient times. In the form of poetic productions, in epics and tales and novels—everywhere, in varied aspects, has been noted this truth. Evidently, popular wisdom has had a premonition as to how often it is needful to remind people both about the necessity of ascent and about the danger of downfall.

Sometimes people ask, "But what then at downfall becomes of all the attained refinements and perceptions? It would certainly seem that the once realized and assimilated could not become non-existent. In what manner are already accomplished attainments displaced into an abased state?"

Such a question is entirely logical and touches upon complex considerations. One has to assimilate very clearly the principle of transformation, both upward and downward. During upward transformation, all possibilities and attainments are, as it were, unrolled; as in a triumphal procession, the banners are unrolled and their inner signs made manifest. Likewise, at transgression and downfall, the banners are rolled up and the things that were recently so gleaming are plunged into profound darkness.

Often people are amazed at the cleverness and the skill of the servants of darkness. But of course, no one has said that they have always been servants of darkness. Perhaps they had taken the downward plunge, about which the above symbol has been given. In the downfall, their attainments had been rolled up and transformed downward. True, their cleverness remained, but it had been changed into evil. During ascent, everything encountered, everything recognized is transformed into good. And just precisely in the opposite process, everything already attained is changed into evil, is changed into injury. It will darken, confuse, and turn into chaos.

In the end, it is not so difficult, even for human reason, to scrutinize what is proceeding toward manifestation and creation, and what toward dissolution and chaos. Precisely as it has been said, "Examine the sum total and then each particularity will stand out conspicuously."

But judgment in perspective does not come so easily. What wise rulers they were, who left behind them the saying: "To govern means to anticipate." Yet in order to anticipate, one has to be able to see into the distance. Even so, some may be confused and mistake a distinction of horizon for self-exaltation, for an excuse to boast of his present cognitions.

If foresight and illumination can be rapidly acquired, just as speedily may come obfuscation and confusion. All of a sudden, man can discover a treasure, but so many times it has happened that people also lose their treasure suddenly and irrevocably.

A great artist and worker told me about how he lost a ring, which he valued very much, in a perfectly definite place, on a smooth seashore where there were no passersby. In his own words, he shifted every grain of sand in this place. He made note of the place and went over it repeatedly, but he never found his memorable ring. And another case is well-known, when a valued ring unexpectedly disappeared in a house and after three weeks was found glittering on the velvet seat of a divan.

Both discoveries and losses are very remarkable if we consider them together with their surroundings.

The possibility of ascent—can it make a man conceited? It does not. It makes him observant, courageous, and untiring. The danger of descent—can it turn a man into a suspicious coward, a tremulous fugitive? It does not. It only sharpens his memory, multiplies his circumspectness, and reminds him how joyful it is to hasten ahead. It is possible to adduce from different literature beautiful words devoted to the great concept, "forward."

Action continuously carried on precisely protects one against many dangers. An arrow does not so easily reach one who is striving impetuously. He passes between the terrors without noticing them, and he increases and preserves his forces by his immutable aspiration. In his striving, there will be no needless luxury. In his striving, he refers good-naturedly to the jostling in the unavoidable crowd. In his impetuousness, he more easily forgives much, which for a loiterer is the object of endless carpings.

Likewise, it was said long ago that in action it is easier to pardon. Of course, in general, this accustoms one to one of the most beneficent qualities, that of forgiveness. The blossoms of forgiveness are beautiful, but a garden of affronts is an extremely repulsive spectacle. The commensurateness of great responsibility, of great preparedness for labor, and, in general, of large measures will also yield great effects. Any limitation, whether it emanates from inconsiderateness, light-mindedness, indolence, immobility—no matter which—will still continue to grow steadily.

The progressions of growths are remarkable. In all the laws of motion can be seen the same basis. So, too, the progression of thinking or of not thinking, of seeing or of not seeing—all this moves and grows exactly the same. Courage, a quality that can be grown, is also multiplied in action. Just as quickly can fear be multiplied—a shameful timorousness, which is terribly dominant in inaction.

Whoever placed upon the rings the spirals of ascent and descent wished to remind continually about the possibilities, both upward and downward. It would seem that if descent is so often mentioned, people would have to take every precaution in order to avoid it. But it does not work out that way in life.

Amid the loftiest and most beautiful symbols, people manage to make objects that tell no one anything about life. And, therefore, in the movements of life itself, so terrible is the necrosis, the vulgarization, which is embedded in the whole meaning of existence, that it dominates the entire tenor of thought and leaves upon everything its infamous seal. Those who observe this would be pessimists, if they should think only about this side. But surely the first spiral, that of ascent, must remain the first, the most attractive and the most inspiring.

Descending from a mountain always produces a sort of sadness, but the ascent is attended with great joy.

When we speak of ascent, we always have before us two powerful, lofty examples: Sri Ramakrishna and Swami Vivekananda. The very fact of the existence of such giants of thought is already a true benefaction for mankind. How many sufferers have found, often by unexpected ways, relief in the sayings and writings of these great sages, and thus a new ascent had its beginning. People should be full of gratitude to those who, by their example, led them to the summits.

ETERNAL LIFE

IN his book, *The Fear of the Dead in Primitive Religion*, George Fraser brings in the wise words of the Omaha tribe about death: "No one can avoid death, and no one must fear death, since it is unavoidable." Likewise, the ancient Mayans calmly said, "I go to rest." If we remember the words of Socrates before his departure, before draining the cup of poison; or the thoughts of Plato and even Epicurus about death, not to speak of the lofty attitude toward this act in the teachings of India, we see the same reasoned, wise consciousness about death as about the alteration of existence. We see the same consciousness of eternal life, which is so cleanly enjoined by the sacred Covenants.

Meanwhile, in the confused minds of the West, particularly in the eighteenth and nineteenth centuries when negation laid its dark path, we see a sort of animal terror in the face of the natural change of existence. Even recently this could be written about, as the intellectual de Sevigné expressed herself: "Death is so fearful, that I hate life more for the reason that it leads to death, rather than for "the thorns with which the path of life is sown." The idea of death poisoned life for Alphonse Daudet, Zola, Goncourt, Maupassant, and other apparently fearless and broad thinkers.

At the same time among people living close to nature, the word "death" is not generally employed. They say, "He has departed," or "He has passed away," meaning that he has terminated this cycle of existence. People in contact with nature are in contact with the basic teachings of truth:

People, being made natural thinkers, likewise naturally understand the significance of a change of being. Fear of death, it would seem, could only arise in malefactors who darken their consciousness with crimes and intentional wrongdoing. It is fully understood that each traitor fears such a striking change of existence. Indeed, within himself he entirely understands that he is being plunged not into non-existence but into some other form of existence. If in his present existence, he has overburdened his heart with quantities of dark purposes and actions, then, indeed, he does not know if it will be easy for him in some conditions unknown to him. Doing unworthy deeds yesterday, man tries to avoid responsibility for them. Such terror at the unavoidable passage into the unknown world is fully understood by people who have darkened their earthly existence with heinous deeds, either material or mental. Surely, it is not necessary to repeat again that thought will be even more potent than word or muscular movement.

Does it not seem strange that, along with criminal beings, certain apparently broad thinkers have also fallen into an animal-like terror before a change of existence? One would like to know if they easily changed their earthly homes. Perhaps, too, on the earth, some of them were not easily moved about. It is well-known that some people believe they can create and think only in their long-occupied domestic environment. Each unusual surrounding already hinders them in expressions of their creativeness. But surely it would seem that precisely diverse impressions and unforeseen experiences and dangers must sharpen thinking, resourcefulness, and boldness. According to courageousness, you can form an opinion about many other qualities of a man. But, of course, courage is tested not by sitting by the stove but there where conflict is encountered with the elements, with darkness, and with all ignorance.

Each one has had an occasion to see people who at a tranquil dinner table employed the boldest speech; but when found face to face with those dangers, about which they were just now speaking so bombastically, they showed themselves in a completely different light. Probably if one speaks with these people about death, they will generally say, "Why speak about such terrible subjects?" This means that they doubt in the goal-fitness of the Universe, with all the strikingly inspiring changes of existence. Apparently they have heard enough about the fact that everything is found to be in motion. It would seem that the newest discoveries would demonstrate sufficiently the fullness of space, and for all that, they are frightened at such a significant and solemn passage into a world new for them. Even for trivial earthly journeys, they will make their wills, not only because they are exceptionally solicitous of someone, but also because, for them, this act is thought of inseparably with the fear of death.

Non-religious people confronted with death hasten away after the completion of rituals. When, in their opinion, the danger has passed, they are the first to relate a blasphemous anecdote. In a recent issue of the magazine *Twentieth Century,* among some very interesting opinions about the ideas and realities of the twentieth century, Professor A. R. Badya, says, "The world is losing the sense of religious values. In its revolt against petrified beliefs and meaningless ceremonies, it falls into the danger of casting out the child along with the bath water. In its suspicion of religions, it is made blind to the meaning and significance of religion." Thus, the learned professor correctly judges and refers carefully to the higher values. In reality, to use the current saying, many children have already been poured out with the bath water. But, of course, among these lightminded outpourings, humanity has cast out precisely that which could strengthen it in creativeness both mental and material.

He who knows about eternal life, by this very fact knows also his joyous responsibility for each action, mental and muscular. In prayers is introduced this great significance of the words "eternal life." He who thinks upon this understands that life is always multiform, both in the horizontal and vertical sense! Even according to primary physical laws, he understands that each minute everything is altered and never arrives again at the former state. In this movement is contained the greatest creative generosity. And how joyful and beneficent the obligation to participate according to one's strength in this all-inclusive creativeness!

Rousseau observes: "He who affirms that he meets death calmly and without fear is simply a liar." Why the great writer Rousseau took it upon himself to speak for all humanity is that he himself must have been afraid of death. Indeed, this act goes beyond the limits of commonplaceness. Therefore, it must be met with a special tranquility of the heart. This consciousness will be far indeed from the so-called calmness before the taking of daily food or any everyday action. But, precisely, in a particular, inspired tranquility, when facing the great change of existence, one will discover a very real magnanimity, which always goes together with wisdom.

The Apostle said clearly and briefly, "We do not die, but are changed." Here, in a few words, is contained the attestation of eternal life. And you remember the words of the Bhagavad Gita about the invisibility, unchangeableness, and eternity of Being. In all ages, in all the ends of the world has eternal life been solemnly and triumphantly confirmed. It means there must have been some unnatural, violent shocks to lead humanity into such an ignorant understanding of the act of the change of existence. At the same time, people begin to speak about life on other planets about which, only recently, even notable astronomers merely shrugged their shoulders. We remember how, for such affirmations, Flammarion was threatened with a loss of scientific standing and with being placed in a class of amateurs. But as of now, the better scientific authorities refer far more cautiously to such recognitions of eternal life.

Indeed, such a basic concept may be perceived only in affirmation. Each ignorant doubt imposes on this clear affirmation well-nigh incurable cleavages. It is deplorable to see when intelligent thinkers fear death and, with that, infect the ignorant masses. Why are they not imbued with that luminous knowledge that belonged to the most ancient wisdom and was confirmed by the best thinkers of all ages? In accordance with the best, you, too, arrive at the best.

THE SUPERNATURAL

THE harmless potato was once known as the "devil's apple," and was a source of riots, war, and banishment. Vaccination was once known as "the sign of the Antichrist." Many physicians have departed this life in martyrdom, and still we have murders, riots, and exile.

Disinfection against plagues and cholera was often regarded as the devil's handiwork and also brought about murders, riots, and exile. And not only the potato and vaccination, but Edison's phonograph was also called charlatanism. One might go on adding to this debauchery of ignorance. Any genuine progress or invention is likely to be called the seal of the Antichrist, the devil's artifice, or charlatanism.

Enlightenment has always been the crying need. Even today, not only in Tibet but in certain parts of America, the earth is thought to be as flat as a plate.

When you begin to explain the sphericity and cite the case of navigation, you will be told, "You can circumnavigate from east to west. But from north to south, it is impossible."

On the one hand, we have flights into the stratosphere and plans to send rockets to the moon, and on the other, the belief that the world is flat and poised like a plate on the horns of a bull. When the bull grows tired and tosses the world from one horn to the other, then we experience an earthquake. All this is quite clear and evident.

The Inquisitors did not trust Galileo in his statement on the revolving of the Earth globe. Salomon de Caus was placed into an insane asylum because of his belief in the power of steam.

Fulton was ridiculed even by his own brother. Galileo wrote with grief that professors in Padua refused to acknowledge anything concerning the planets, the moon, and even the telescope, and that they were searching for truth not in the world or in nature but by comparing texts and trying to deprive the sky of planets by logical proofs.

Two hundred years later, Hegel, basing himself on philosophical proofs, tried to demonstrate the impossibility of the existence of planets between Jupiter and Mars. But in the very same year, Piazzi discovered the first dwarf planet. Auguste Comte denied the possibility of analyzing the chemical nature of stars. Five years later, the inventors of spectral analysis established the classification of stars according to their chemical constituents.

Arago, Thiers, Proudhon were unable to push through the future of railways. Thomas Young and Fresnel were publicly ridiculed by Lord Brougham because of their discovery of the wave theory.

In 1878, Bouillot, a member of the institute, witnessing the demonstration of Edison's phonograph by du Moncel before the French Academy, declared that this was only a trick and, half a year later, urged the Academy not to trust "American charlatans."

And so, with the transmission of thought at a distance, Bekhterev, who worked on this problem, was called a madman; and even today, when scores of university professors are engaged in successful experiments in thought transmission, there are still many who persist in considering it a matter of dark superstition. They are not hampered by the question as to what sort of spiritism, since the interchange takes place between living persons. Though Prof. Rhine at Duke University has succeeded in convincing the elite by through his remarkable experiments in thought transference, there are, nonetheless, a mass of ignorant people who would like to cast doubt about his work. Whole volumes have been written on the martyrdom of scholars and artists.

People will have to realize someday that the supernatural is not inexistent, and that there is only the known and the, as yet, unknown. The brilliant discoveries of recent years ought to lead humanity toward reason.

SYNTHESIS

IT would seem that the entire history of humanity directs us once and forever to understand the principles of cooperation, containment, and the harmonization of the centers.* But reality shows that things are entirely different. I will not reiterate about the obvious dark forces, to whom every mention about synthesis is adverse and irritating. This is quite natural for chaos, with all its disorderly whirls, which is opposed to harmony, progress, and constructiveness. Thus, we will not be surprised that darkness always is and will be against every constructiveness and synthesis. But it is especially deplorable when one witnesses that even certain seemingly cultural minds are disturbed and revolt against every reference to synthesis. Such a slight is so unexpectedly rude and vulgar that one does not even want to believe that under the masks of respectability and sweet voices could hide such fossilized and dusty, outlived ideas. Darkness hopes to break up the light, but encounters are defeated in such absurd attempts. All voluntary and involuntary allies of darkness are also certainly defeated in due course. But time is needed to find out every absurdity. It is infinitely sad to witness how valuable, irreplaceable time is wasted on mutual negations and divisions in order not to admit the possibility of healthy, blissful synthesis.

If we will tell ourselves that this deplorable state is the consequence of darkness, it will be a poor consolation. Or if we say that it issues from narrow thinking or envy

---

* Nerve centers.

or malice, then this will be a still poorer consolation because such abhorrent properties are also created by the same darkness. The spreading of darkness is terrible, and it ravages like a pernicious epidemic. Humanity has discovered many salutary remedies against plague, cholera, and similar pestilences, but the microbes of dark negation still have not been found.

Turning to the history of humanity, we see a multitude of examples of the most absurd negations, with the sole purpose to besmirch constructive synthesis. Many stupidities were expressed to the effect that Leonardo da Vinci harmed his great art by being at the same time a remarkable engineer, biologist, and philosopher. And more than once it was hinted, in the most ignorant way, that the art of Rubens suffered from his diplomatic career and statesmanship. However, a mighty creativeness and a wide mind demand multifarious expressions in varied materials and domains. The ordainments of Eastern wisdom tell us that even Bodhisattvas should master at least one art and one craft. The wisdom of ancient rabbis underlines that if the youth, besides its main activity, will not be skilled in some craft, then it will be like preparing them for the banditry of the crossroads.

The whole of antiquity, all epochs of renaissance relate the most striking compatibilities. Let us not forget Cardinal Richelieu, who when searching for an active secretary chose a man who was busy in many fields. And when it was hinted to the cardinal that this man was already too busy for a new appointment, the experienced statesman replied, "If he is so busy, he will know how to also find time for my work." The much-experienced cardinal valued all advantages derived from the realization of synthesis.

We further know that Julius Caesar sometimes dictated six letters simultaneously. Long is the list of such similar examples of containment and compatibilities, which but prove the inexhaustible possibilities of a man.

We heard that Einstein, besides being a brilliant mathematician, is also a wonderful violinist. Has music belittled his astounding mathematical foresight? Certainly not. The harmony of sound gave him new daring thoughts of his definition of the Universe. The remarkable pianist Hoffmann, at the same time, is also an excellent mathematician and engineer. Who will dare to say that one or the other is incompatible and an impeding principle? Spinoza was a skillful master of telescopical lenses and besides was known as a fine portraitist. Has his deep philosophy suffered from this, or have his lenses become worse because of his philosophy?

One may enumerate numerous similar examples, in which a thinker also expressed himself in different fields of creativeness and craftsmanship.

It would seem that these facts are sufficiently obvious and dear and that one needn't dwell on them. But humanity, up to now, strives by all means to affirm the unnecessary divisions and perilous specialization.

The horrors of unemployment, the horrors of the inability to properly assign one's time and capacities are due to such absurd divisions. At the time of the Italian renaissance, Leonardo and many other masters, endowed with various talents, were recognized; but now, in spite of every kind of human progress, this would call forth many negations and condemnations. I was witness to a discussion that took place as to whether the composer Rachmaninov should also appear as a conductor of a symphony orchestra. According to the opinion of a certain manager, a good composer could not also be a good conductor, and *vice versa*. The ideas of the manager were that one should not burden the public with such compatibility. As if the broad masses could in no way understand that a man can act in two fields if they are close to each other in their essence! No doubt the same manager would have condemned Hoffmann for his love for mathematics, or Alexandre Nikolayevich Benois for permitting himself to be at the same time an artist and a writer. No doubt a reference to the famous Italian Vasari, who was both an artist and a historian, would have been of small avail to persuade present-day ignoramuses. Someone even stated the stupidity that an artist cannot be a philosopher—in other words, a clever person—as if creativeness was connected only with idiots; and when it was recently printed in the papers that the Lord Mayor of Bridgeport, who is a skilled roof layer, continued his handicraft even during his municipal activities, then the readers only smiled. From the point of view of the disseminator and the belittler, this was proof of the uselessness of the Lord Mayor in both fields. And what is there bad in the fact that the famous Russian composer Borodin, of *Prince Igor* fame, was a professor of the Military Medical Academy?

Divisions and conventional limitations have reached incredible absurdity. One must have a very poor mind when one directs humanity toward such deadly divisions and prohibitions. Precisely from them is generated a shameful, mutual human hatred, of which we are witness. The study of the nervous system, with its fiery energies, shows what a many-sided instrument the human organism is.

In the name of the highest knowledge, in the name of the betterment of life, in the name of cooperation, we have to acknowledge the hidden properties and possibilities in every human being. And having admitted the existence of these happy qualities, people must find in themselves the moral strength to express themselves, despite the whisperings of darkness, for the good of all, not being held back by prohibition where existence itself commands the possibilities of flourishing containment and synthesis. Especially, let the youth, students from the first days of their studies, hear of synthesis as the true mover of progress.

THE ETERNAL GARMENT

MANY years ago, I had a painting, the subject of which was a woman making her first dress. In this painting were displayed ornaments whose design dated from most ancient times. But the most amazing thing was to see that these ornaments were closely related to the designs that we see today.

You have no doubt also heard of the ancient Scythian art, now in vogue, which is considered the forerunner of Cubism.

In 1922, in Chicago, during the production of the *Snow Maiden*, Marshall Field and Company tried to create some modern costumes employing the styles and ornaments taken from old designs and historic figures. It was really remarkable and very significant to see how some of these models came directly from the most ancient sources of design. It was also astonishing to observe how these historic ornaments had been carried out in a most modern way.

In connection with the expression of the old in the new, I am reminded of the time when, in Tibet, I gave some photographs of skyscrapers to the people. They appreciated them most highly because they, in their own country, had had skyscrapers since the sixteenth century, in such buildings as the Potala, which is seventeen stories in height; and not only were these skyscrapers equally high, but one should realize that in the character of their design, they were in reality the forerunners of our modern skyscrapers. Thus again, we see that the most ancient and the most modern thoughts are being united.

In my diary, I have found a page dedicated to the production of *Le Sacre du Printemps*: "Eighteen years have elapsed since, with Stravinsky, we sat in the colorful fairy house, Talashkino, in Smolensk, the estate of Princess Maria Klavdievna Tenisheva, working on the scheme of *Le Sacre du Printemps*. And Princess Tenisheva asked us to write on the beams of this multicolored house some excerpts from *Sacre* as a memento. Probably even now, some fragments of our inscriptions remain there. But who knows if the present inhabitants of this house realize what is written there, upon the beams?

"It was a pleasant time when the Church of the Holy Spirit and my painting *Human Forefathers* were completed. The hills of Smolensk and the white birches and the yellow buttercups and white water lilies, like the ancient lotuses of India, reminded us of the Shepherd Lel and Koupava or Krishna and the Gopis. In eternal conceptions as these was interwoven the wisdom of the East with the best images of the West.

"Then war came, and I heard that one of my sketches in Stravinsky's estate as well as the sketches of *Sacre* were destroyed. Many events have passed by but the eternal remains.

"During these years we have witnessed how in all of Asia the eternal rhythm of 'Sacre' resounds in the holy mountains and in the deserts, where the songs are presented not for human beings but for the great desert itself. When a Mongol refused to repeat his beautiful song to us because 'he sang only for the great desert,' we remembered Stravinsky and how he embodied in the symphony of *Sacre*, the eternal rhythm of human striving and the victory of the spirit. In Kashmir, when we admired the majestic sight of the festival of spring, with its gorgeous torch dances, I again recalled the powerful musical concepts of Stravinsky.

"When in the mountain monasteries we heard gigantic trumpets and rejoiced before the sacred dances, full of rhythmic, symbolic movement, again the names of Stravinsky, Stokowski, and Prokofiev came into my mind.

"In Sikkim, at the festivals of homage to the great Kanchenjunga, we felt the same link with the eternal homage to greatness that inspired the best poetical images of Siva, who consumed the poison of the world for the sake of humanity, and of all the great redeemers and heroes, the creators of human ascension.

"During this time, I had already heard that *Sacre* was acclaimed everywhere, and there no longer exists any conventional prejudice against this expression.

"And I remember how, during the first production in Paris, in 1913, the entire audience whistled and roared so that nothing could even be heard. Who knows, perhaps at this very moment they were enjoying themselves with the same emotions of primitive people. But this savage primitiveness had nothing in common with the refined primitiveness of our ancestors, for whom rhythm, the sacred symbol, and refinement of gesture were great and sacred concepts.

"Well, perhaps it was necessary that thousands of years elapse in order that we might witness how humanity would become conventional and how much prejudice would exist between the listener and the fact. At the same time, it is not so easy to approach the facts honestly. Again, our poor egoism, conceit, and conventionality can hinder and shadow reality. But it is so uplifting to feel that in America, during the ten years of activity, I did not sense any cheap chauvinism or bigotry. Perhaps the new combination of nations preserves America from poisonous pettiness, and the heritage of the great culture of the Mayas and Aztecs gave its heroic background to the great movements of this country. Verily, here in America, you do not need to be negative. So many beautiful things are possible if we can keep our positivity and open-mindedness. We can feel how the primal energy is electrified in this country, and through this energy, in the easiest way, you can reach the inner constructive feeling of the nation. This constructive striving of spirit, this joy before the beautiful laws of nature and heroic sacrifices, are certainly the essential feelings of *Le Sacre du Printemps*. We cannot consider 'Sacre' as Russian, or even Slavic. It is more ancient and panhuman.

"This is the natural festival of the soul. This is the joy of love and self-sacrifice, not under the knife of crude conventionality but in exuberance of the spirit, in connecting our earthly existence with the Supreme.

"On the multicolored house of the Tenisheva estate are inscribed fragments of the *Sacre*. Princess Tenisheva, the self-sacrificing collector and worker in the field of art, has already passed away. Nizhinsky is no longer with us, and already Diaghilev rejoices in higher spheres.

"And still *Sacre* is new, and the young ones are accepting *Sacre* as a new conception; and perhaps the eternal novelty of *Sacre* is because spring is eternal, and love is eternal, and sacrifice is eternal. Thus in this new conception, Stravinsky touches the eternal in music. He was modern because he evoked the future; it is the great serpent ring touching the great past.

"And the wizard of the symphony, Stokowski, with his sensitivity for truth and beauty, with his magic baton, like the eternal priest, again evokes to life the sacred tunes that connect the great past and future.

"The torch festival in Kashmir is so beautiful! So majestic are the gigantic trumpets in the mountain monasteries! And from beyond Kanchenjunga itself began the great migration with the *Eternal Sacre!*"

We know that growth without refinement is undesirable. Everywhere, we see expansion without refinement; this growth will express itself in cruelty and rudeness.

Another thing that is important: When in 1921, in Arizona, I showed some photographs of the Mongols to some Indians, they said: "Oh, they are Indians! They are our brothers!" And similarly, when in Mongolia, I showed the Mongols pictures of the American Indians in Santa Fe, they recognized them as their closest relatives. And they told me a beautiful fairy tale—how at one time, there lived two brothers and how the earth on which they lived was split. And since that time, these relatives have always been expecting news of one another, and they have always been confident that sometime they will receive news of them. Thus, from the most ancient times people look to the future.

When you are in Asia, you see much around you that would be considered here as supernatural. In that country, however, everything is quite natural. We are concerned with the problems that are nearer to life. We dream of having a theater in life. In Asia, they have it. In Mongolia, during the sacred dances, many sacred designs are seen. Many ancient banners and sacred images are seen in the desert—thousands of people, huge orchestras, beautiful costumes, remarkable designs. Everything there is regarded as an expression of life. If you are admitted to participate in this life, you can see no difference between nature and the life of today, and this is a splendid realization.

In answer to the question as to why they had such tremendously long trumpets with such a powerful sound, a lama in Tibet answered that once upon a time a ruler of Tibet wanted to greet a great Teacher from India. The question arose as to how this Teacher should be greeted. He could not be approached with gold, silver, and precious stones. The lama advised the ruler to construct special trumpets in order to greet the Teacher with new, unprecedented sounds. Again here, the beautiful searching seems so similar to the searing of our days.

Remember the designs of the American Indians in the old pueblos? Before the people were divided into separate nations, they probably had only one language. So in trying to unify the national symbols into one, we can quite easily observe a historic symbol of pure design. In this are collected the perpetual symbols of nature. In the rainbow, the lightning, the clouds, we see the history of the striving of expression toward the beautiful—a striving that is the same everywhere. Whether we find that expression in

Russia or in Mongolia or in Arizona, it is all the expression of this great human design.

This should be very close to us all because today we are striving toward the next evolution. We are trying to discard old forms and to create something new. But in order to strive for something new, we have to first know the old. Only then can we attain the true enhancement of life.

Now I hear my friend Léonide Massine, the famous dancer and ballet producer, is preparing a new staging of *Sacre* in the U.S.A. With great difficulty, the new sketches were sent from India. Thus, in this time of Armageddon, humanity again ponders over spring, love, and the beautiful. Let the eternal garment cover the disturbed human mind.

V

GREEN LEAVES

REALIZATION OF THE BEAUTIFUL

P LATO ordained in his treatises on statesmanship:
It is difficult to imagine a better method of education
than that that has been discovered and verified and by the
experience of centuries it can be expressed "in two prop-
ositions: gymnastics for the body and music for the soul."
In view of this one must consider education in music as
the most important; thanks to it Rhythm and Harmony
are deeply inrooted into the soul, dominate it, fill it with
beauty and transform man into a beautiful thinker. He
will partake of the Beautiful and rejoice at it, gladly realize it, become saturated with it and will arrange his life in
conformity with it.

Of course, the word "music," in this case, should not
be understood as routine musical education, as it is understood now in its narrow sense. Music had in Athens, as a
service to all the Muses, a far deeper and broader meaning
than today. This conception embraced not only the harmony of sound but the whole domain of poetry, the whole
domain of high perceptions, of exquisite forms and creation in general, in its best sense. The great service to the
Muses was a real education of taste, which in everything
cognizes the great Beautiful. Just to this eternal Beauty in
all its vitality, we have to revert, if only the ideas of high
constructiveness are not rejected by humanity.

Hippias Maior (beauty) of the dialogue of Plato is not a
hazy abstractness but verily the most vital noble conception. The Beautiful in itself! The perceptible and conceivable! In this reality is contained an inspiring, encouraging
welcome to the study and inrooting of all ordainments of

the Beautiful. "The philosophic moral" of Plato is animated by the sense of the beautiful. And did not Plato himself, who was sold into slavery through the hatred of the tyrant Dionysius and when liberated and dwelling in the gardens of the Academy, prove through his example the vitality of a beautiful path? Of course, Plato's gymnastics were not the coarse football or anticultural breaking of noses of modern prizefights. The gymnastics of Plato were the same gates to the Beautiful—the discipline of harmony and uplifting of the body into the spiritual spheres.

Not once have we spoken about the introduction in school of a chair of ethics of life, a course of the art of thinking. Without the education of the general realization of the beautiful, these two courses will again remain a dead letter. Again, in the course of only a few years, the high vital principles of ethics will turn into a dead dogma if they are not imbued with the Beautiful.

Many vital conceptions of antiquity have become in our household belittled and vulgar instead of the deserved expansion. Thus the all-embracing, wide and lofty service to the Muses turned into a narrow conception of playing one instrument. When you hear nowadays the word music, you imagine first of all a lesson of music often with conventional limitations. When one hears the word "museum," one understands it as a storeroom of any kind of art objects. As every storehouse, this conception creates a certain flavor of deadliness. Such limited conception of the word "museum" as a storage place, so deeply entered our understanding that when one pronounces this conception in its original meaning—muzeon—then no one understands what is really meant. Yet every Hellene of even average education would at once know that Muzeon means first of all the Home of the Muses.

Primarily, Muzeon is the abode of all aspects of the Beautiful—not at all in the sense of storing only different kinds of art creations but in the sense of the most vital and creative application of them in life. Thus one hears often nowadays that people express surprise when a Museum, as such, occupies itself with all spheres of Art, occupies itself with the education of good taste and with the spreading of the sense of the Beautiful.

Here we remember the ordainments of Plato. But in the same way, one may also remember Pythagoras with his Laws of the Beautiful, with his adamant foundations of cosmic realizations. The ancient Hellenes went so far as to crown their Pantheon with an altar to the Unknown God. In this exaltation of spirit they came close to the refined inexpressible conception of the ancient Hindus, who pronouncing *"Neti, neti"* by no means wanted to say anything negative, but on the contrary, by saying "not this, not this" manifested thereby the untold greatness of an inexpressible concept.

It is significant that such great conceptions were not abstract, as if living only in the mind and reason: no, they dwelled in the very heart as something living, life-bringing, inalienable and indestructible, as defined so beautifully in the *Bhagavad Gita*. In the heart was aflame that sacred fire, which was at the base of all flaming commandments and also of the hermits of Mt. Sinai. The same sacred fire molded the precious images of St. Theresa, St. Francis, St. Sergius, and all the Fathers of the "Love of the Good," who knew so much and were understood so little.

We speak of the education of good taste, as of a matter of truly basic world significance of every country. When we speak about vital ethics, which should become the favorite school hour of every child, we appeal to the contemporary heart, pleading to it for expansion, if even only to the extent of ancient ordainments.

Can one consider as natural the fact that the conception already so glorified in the time of Pythagoras and Plato has been so narrowed now and lost its actual meaning, after all the ages of so-called progress? Pythagoras even in the fifth century BC symbolized in himself the whole harmonious "Pythagorean Life." It was Pythagoras who affirmed music and astronomy as sisters in science. Pythagoras, who was called by bigots a charlatan, must be horrified to see how, instead of showing a harmonious development, our contemporary life has been broken up and mutilated, and that we do not even understand the meaning of the beautiful hymn to the sun—to Light.

Today very strange formulae sometimes appear in the press. For instance, that the flourishing of the intellect is the sign of degeneration. A very strange formula, if only the author does not attribute to the word "intellect" some special narrow meaning. Of course, if the word "intellect" is only taken as the expression of the conventional withered mind, then to some extent this formula may have its foundation. But it is dangerous in case the author understands intellect as intelligence, which first of all should be connected with the education of good taste as the most vital principle of life.

Quite recently before our eyes, in the West has been adopted a new word—intelligentsia. In the beginning this newcomer was met rather suspiciously, but soon it was adopted in literature. It would be important to determine whether this expression symbolizes the intellect or, according to ancient conceptions, it corresponds to the education of good taste.

If it is a symbol of a refined and expanded consciousness, then we have to greet this innovation, which perhaps will remind us once more of the ancient beautiful principles.

In my letter "Synthesis," the difference of conceptions of Culture and Civilization were discussed. Both these conceptions are sufficiently separated, even in standard dictionaries. Let us not, therefore, return to these two consecutive conceptions, even if someone would be content with the conception of civilization without dreaming about the higher conception of culture.

But remembering about "intelligentsia," it is permissible to ask whether this conception belongs to Civilization, as to the expression of intellect, or whether it does already touch a higher region, that is to say, whether it belongs to the region of Culture, in which the heart and spirit already act. Of course, if we assume that the expression "intelligentsia" should remain only within the limitation of the mind, then there would be no need to burden it with our literary vocabulary. One may permit an innovation only in such cases when something really new is introduced or at least when ancient principles are renewed in present modern circumstances.

Of course, everyone will agree that intelligentsia, this aristocracy of the Spirit, belongs to Culture, and only in this connection could one greet this new literary expression.

In this case, the education of good taste belongs, first of all, of course, to the intelligentsia, and not only does it belong, but it becomes its duty. Without fulfilling this duty, intelligentsia has no right for existence and condemns itself to savagery.

The education of good taste cannot be something abstract, where above all, this is a vital attainment in all spheres of life, for can there be a boundary to the service to the Muses of the ancient Hellenes? If in the old days this service was understood in its full glory and adapted to life in the whole beauty of its principle, then should we not be ashamed, if in superstition and bigotry we cut off the radiant wings of the rising spirits?

When we propose ethics as a course in schools, as a theme most inspiring, limitless, full of constructive principles, we thus, presuppose, at the same time, the transmutation of taste as a defense against vulgarity and ugliness.

Andromeda said: "And I brought thee the Fire!" The ancient Hellene, the follower of Euripides, understood the meaning of this Fire and why this Agni is so precious. We, however, in most cases babble about this inspiring conception as about phosphor matches. We attach the high conception of Phosphor—the bringer of Light—to a match and try to light with it our extinguished hearth in order to prepare the broth for today. But where is Tomorrow, this radiant wonderful Tomorrow?

We have forgotten about it. We have forgotten because

we have lost the ability of searching, have lost the refined taste that urges to betterment, to dreams, to higher consciousness. Dreams have become like dull slumber; but he who does not know how to dream does not belong to the future, does not belong to humanity with its high ideal.

Even the simple truth that dreams about the future are the basic distinction of man from animal has already become a truism. But a truism in itself is no longer a generally accepted truth, as it should be, but has become the synonym of a truth of which one should not think altogether. Nevertheless, disregarding everything, even in times of the greatest difficulties and world crises, let us not defer the thought about the education of taste; let us not put off the thought of life-bringing ethics as of a necessary course of school education. Let us not forget the art of thinking, the art of memory, and let us forever remember the treasure of the heart.

A certain hermit left his retreat and came with the message, saying to everyone: "Thou hast a heart." When he was asked why he does not speak about mercy, patience, devotion, love, and all the other benevolent foundations of life, he replied: "If only they do not forget the heart, the rest will adjust itself." Verily can we appeal for love if it has no place to reside? And where can patience dwell when its abode is closed? Thus in order not to torture ourselves with inapplicable blisses, we must build that garden that will flourish in the realization of the heart. Let us stand firmly on the foundation of the heart, and let us understand that without the heart we are as a lost shell." Thus the Wise Ones ordained. Thus ordains *Agni Yoga*. Thus let us accept and apply.

Without the untiring realization of the Beautiful, without incessant refinement of the heart and consciousness, we would make the laws of earthly existence cruel and deadly in their hatred against humanity. In other words, we would, when killing the Beautiful, assist the most shameful, debased downfall.

The Romans said: *Sub pretextu juris summum jus saepe summa injuria; suaviter in modo fortiter in re.* ("Under the pretext of justice, a strict application of law is often the gravest injury. Be gentle in manner, though resolute in execution.")

Let us be broad and resolute in the realization of the Beautiful!

Vivekananda said, "The artist is the witness of the Beautiful."

Rabindranath Tagore finishes his article *What Is Art?* with such words:

"In Art the person in us is sending its answer to the Supreme Person, who reveals Himself to us in a world of endless beauty across the lightless world of facts."

There is no other way, O friends scattered! May my call penetrate to you. Let us join ourselves by the invisible threads of the Beautiful. I turn to you, I call to you; in the name of Beauty and Wisdom, let us combine for struggle and work.

During the days of Armageddon, let us ponder on Eternal Values, which are the cornerstone of Evolution.

In the name of Culture, I send you from the Himalayas my heartiest greetings!

VICTORY OF THOUGHTS

A NEWSPAPER reports:
"Record of human thought—Experiment of two Cambridge Professors."—"Two Professors of the Cambridge University have succeeded in making cinema photographs of human thought. One of them is Dr. Adrian, Professor of Physiology and a distinguished Member of the Royal Society, the other is Prof. Mathews. Adrian, who has dedicated his whole life to the investigation of the mysteries of the nervous system, in 1932 received the Nobel Prize and only a few days back was awarded the Gold Medal of the Royal Society."

"When a person sits quietly in a chair with closed eyes and his thought is not occupied with anything serious, then his brain matter produces regular electrical discharges at the rate of about ten discharges per second. With the help of very complicated and ingenuous apparati and a photo-electric camera, Prof. Adrian succeeded in registering these discharges on a cinema-film. He likewise observed that as soon as his patient opens his eyes and begins to concentrate his attention on something, the frequency of discharges increases considerably and reaches usually about 2,000 per sec."

"The rhythmic impulses continue also during deep sleep and also when the person (or animal) is subjected to the influence of narcotics. The professor proved by experimental methods the similarity of vibrations in different persons of the sight of the same object or manifestation. Different thoughts, which arise as a consequence of the action of the visual nerves, give different impressions upon the film.

"Prof. Adrian confined his experiments mainly to that part of the human brain which controls vision. He proved that this region of the brain is extraordinarily small. And Prof. Adrian established the fact with the help of his apparati that the greater part of the human brain does not participate in any mental process.

"Prof. Adrian carried his experiments to such a degree of perfection that he can now easily change his photographic records of thought into sound and can broadcast it over the radio for the public. During a public demonstration the audience heard a great variety of sounds, varying with the visual impressions of the patient, who sat upon the stage and opened his eyes at the direction of the professor."

Thus something quite natural and perhaps long ago known is already being recorded already by crude mechanical apparati. Long before these mechanical records were achieved, the great Indian scholar Sir Jagadis Bose in similar experiments recorded the pulse of plants and demonstrated even for a casual observer, how plants react to pain and light and how the appearance of even a distant cloud reacts upon the pulse. Graphically he showed on a screen the agony of a plant's death, poisoned or transfixed. At the same time, he recorded the influence of human energy upon the life of the same plants, which not long ago were in the eyes of civilized people regarded to be but mere lower growths, devoid of any senses.

By the movement of the needle, which records the pulse of the plant, one can notice the influence of human energy of thought. A kind thought, a sympathetic thought could protect the plant from the action of poison. In the same degree, a hostile thought would increase the fatal action.

If only quicker, as quickly as possible, the realization of the importance and power of thought would penetrate into the minds of even the uneducated masses! It is ridiculous and humiliating to subject that lofty experiment upon human thought to the action of coarse mechanical apparatuses. But for a coarse consciousness, similar methods of investigation are necessary. The realization alone of the significance of thought would already considerably transform our earthly existence.

In the realm of television, important, purely mechanical improvements take place. It has just been reported that during the current year, this transmission of vision at a distance will receive new possibilities. This is quite possible since once the field has been entered, the results in this direction will no doubt accumulate shortly. Gradually the reflection of the quality of thought will also become apparent through television, when images of persons are transmitted.

Even some observant photographers point out that the difference of photographs depends not only on purely external conditions but also on the inner state of the subject. Thus also in this case we arrive at the concept of the reflection of thought.

Discussions about hypnotism and suggestion, that is to say about the trained methods of influence, have already become common. But the limited consciousness as yet but feebly admits that not only in cases of trained mental influences but absolutely cases of more or less clear thinking, powerful reactions upon the surroundings take place.

This consideration will once more remind us of the concept of responsibility, about which we recently had several evidences. What lofty beauty is contained in the idea of responsibility and service! And there is no such spot on earth where man would not be subject to these two great predestinations.

When we evoke from space words and sounds, are they not also followed by the ever-present properties of the energy of thought? Along tremendous distances the human voice, directed by thought, clearly resounds.

No doubt, across vast space together with the outer Sound are also stretched the inner strings of a mighty energy. Some will sense them quite clearly; another, though feeling them, will deny. And in such a negation there will be again present the element of fear. For the fearing consciousness shudders at the very hint that it is surrounded by influences and energies. Precisely that which should uplift people casts the weak- willed into fear. Precisely into fear, which is the consequence of something indefinite and chaotic. But fear will not save us from chaos. Fears are the very gates to chaos!

It is beautiful, being clad in valor, to realize the grandeur of thought and of all the energies that it sets into action. Though through mechanical means, nevertheless let people hurriedly approach the thoughts about thought in all its mighty significance. And instead of a chaotic fear, many seemingly complicated problems of life will become illumined by the realization of all the possibilities of thought. Not without reason was it said: "Act not only in body, but also in thought!"

What a beautiful concept: "Thought in Infinity."

ROBOTS

"ERIC, the robot, was exhibited for the first time in England at the Schoolboy Exhibition. It can fire a machine gun at command."

This is the caption under a photograph of a steel monster, which appeared in one of the local newspapers. In the rotogravure section of the *New York Times* is depicted a scientist from Massachusetts making some complicated calculations, and the caption says that he is inventing brains for a robot. Thus, in all corners of the world, humanity is not preoccupied with devices of self-perfection but is busy with perfecting monsters that could replace man in various fields. Thus, the very quality of man's labor is substituted in our civilized world by the conventional properties of soulless automatons.

Many millions of the unemployed and hungry ones are in search of labor, ready to apply their energy and skill to any work, only to be saved from want and hunger. But they are threatened not only by living competitors, but brains are even being invented for some robots. It is possible that all calamities and malicious confusions of man's trend of thought will be directed chiefly along the lines of soulless mechanization, forgetting the true meaning of their earthly destination!

Music is canned, art is on film, lectures are on the radio, ships run without captains, bombing airplanes fly without a pilot, and as a climax of mechanization and the crown of the annihilation of the human spirit stands a war of poisonous gases and biological extermination of all that lives. The old ordainment of "all living should live" begins to appear as something out of date. Instead of mighty symphonies and inspiring operas, the saxophone is howling and men move slowly in the mechanical *macabre*.

We want to think that this is an exaggeration. Perhaps the invasion of robots under various garbs and marks is not as threatening, but to this effect testify many newspapers and communications from all parts of the world. From everywhere reach us wailings not only about unemployment but also about the deadening of the spirit. The inspiring spiritual leader T. L. Vaswani regrets the rapidly growing tendency to cynicism. He points out that hero worship is the basis of an individual's advance and a nation's progress. Cynicism is a form of disintegration. Our need is a new integration of thought and life. He rightly refers to cynics as "crows." Hero worship is the "spring of national life."

From a different part of the world echoes: "We want heroism that is heroic in its own secret thoughts. We want heroes who slay dragons in private. We want royal courage that strangles an unworthy impulse as soon as it is born . . . It must be in his nature to be heroic."

And we also hear: "Look around. There is depression. There is despair. We need reconstruction, regeneration, rejuvenation. The ancient book prayed: *"Tamaso ma jyotir gamaya."* "Through darkness, lead us unto light." Yes, the path to light passes through the realm of suffering and sorrow!" Verily, this path is being fulfilled. Darkness has become so dense that people, drowning in it, cease to desire light. Under the eyes of the hungry, hecatombs of grain are being burnt. Millions of cattle are being destroyed in order to clear them out of the way for some kind of speculation, and it is argued that some people who will remain will derive an unusual benefit from this procedure. But who will it be? Who will survive and remain? And will he not then encounter some long ago, wound-up robot, and will the latter not smash his head by his usual mechanical movement, while the last mechanical record finishes playing a jazz piece on the theme of Chopin's *Funeral March*?

At the same time, despite all these terrible signs, we cannot be pessimists. We know that the robots will manifest themselves in all their mechanical ignorance. Precisely, they, as it has already happened, will stop traffic. They will not deliver an urgent message; they, rusty from fog, will steer the ship toward a fatal rock. It is difficult to imagine who will prove to be more destructive—the robots wound by a mechanical hand or that anticipated, inhuman biological war that is discussed in the newspapers.

Perhaps some people hope that nothing will remain of our civilization altogether, not to mention our culture. But then the shameful pages of newspapers with their columns about crimes would decay at first turn. I recollect how H. G. Wells, making a speech at a dinner, said: "Do not be surprised if this piece of glass becomes a rarity someday for somebody!" This joke expressed a genuine irony in regard to a sad reality.

And still, above all robots, above all vipers of godlessness and dark ignorance, beautiful hearts of cooperation are born. True, they are rare. It is also true that everyone who enters this path encounters many difficulties. Black stones are showered at him. All robots and man-haters would like to see destroyed everyone who thinks of creative cooperation. There is not even a shadow of a possibility for the dark ones to convert to their faith or rather atheism, those young ones devoted to the true cognizance of the heart. Therefore, darkness condemns them to annihilation, and there is no such malevolent invention and slander that would lose the opportunity to destroy each ray of light.

But the ancient Rishis have foreseen precisely this hour of darkness, which is the testing stone for those in quest of the Light. These seekers of the good know these obstacles are not accidental and must be conquered. Amid true seekers, there are also many pseudo-seekers. There are many of those Nicodemuses of the night who whisper sweet words at night and are ready to betray in daytime.

Give them the smallest test to express their own tendencies, and at once they will disappear into the abyss from where they came.

Ask whether this Nicodemus would sacrifice for the sake of a good night's sleep, and he will hasten to disappear in order not to burden himself with the slightest effort. But man lives not for them. People live for the sake of those devoted hearts, the mere mentioning of which multiplies one's strength. Those who cling to darkness will abide with it, but those in quest of the Light will reach it despite all dark obstacles.

The Fiery World ordains: "Let him rather think of the purification of his heart. Let him not imagine himself as the conqueror of Cosmos, but let him desire to purify his consciousness from dust. One cannot penetrate beyond the boundaries of the law without the desire to approach it transfigured. Precisely the baker of spiritual and physical bread must not think as how to satiate himself. . . ."*

"Amid psychic diseases, the most disagreeable and almost incurable are treason and sacrilege. Once a traitor, always a traitor. Only the strongest fiery blow can purify such contaminated brains. If such a criminal state occurs from obsession, such cause is not consoling either. Can one imagine cooperation with a traitor or one who commits sacrilege? They are like a plague in the house."**

My friends, many robots are at work now. There are all kinds of conventionalities, deadening forbiddances, and rusty creakings of wrath, and all other properties of mechanization and all kinds of technocracies—all these dark evils will be conquered by the fiery heart. When I think of you who gather in friendship in the name of true peace and cooperation, my heart always fills with joy. Working all day, giving your energy sometimes to routine work, you find strength to gather in the evening with all the vitality of the spirit for uplifting spiritual deeds.

---

* From *Fiery World II*, verse 442.
** Ibid., verse 445.

Honor to those who inspire you to strive to these achievements; honor to you who find within yourselves the indefatigability and patience to transmute the routine of life into a radiant, beautiful garden.

FREDUM

FREDUM is the term given in the ancient laws of the Franks to the fine imposed against the violation of peace. In other words, this fine is the "cost of peace," or "price of peace." Other similar fines were "the cost of man," or "the cost of blood," or "the cost of vengeance," also known as *wergeld* and *fuidu*; *fredum*, among all these laws, is also one of greatest significance for our times. We should not be surprised that under current circumstances so-called civilized mankind has something yet to learn, even from the ancient Franks.

The people who considered it necessary to safeguard by law a peaceful state of life were striving to ethical legal codes. It would also be good if nowadays amid the numerous international, criminal, and civil laws, people remember the basic question of the violation of peace. Such a law could remind people in everyday life of the significance of this imperative concept. Everyone wants peace. But— *horribile dictu*—many wish to approach it not by peaceful means. But true peace cannot be built on the foundations of insult, belittling, or self-glorification.

In all aspects of life, the concept of human dignity should always, of course, be venerated and upheld. People should not only be conscious of but learn to love the concepts of dignity, honor, and heroic attainment. These qualities should not be abstract, as on the stage or in the pages of novels. They should be manifested in all the details of daily life. They should be vital because only living is convincing.

One sometimes hears nowadays that the concepts of

honor and dignity are considered as outlived. And around the word "honor," there seem to hover duels, bloody fights, and mutual assaults. But honor has nothing in common with the bloodshed of a duel. The human consciousness should, of course, be superior to the "price of blood." A righteous judgment need not be based on walking upon red-hot iron. It is never permissible to combine the living concepts of honor and dignity with certain medieval conventionalities.

It is quite possible that timid thinking is afraid to include in contemporary life many concepts, which are as if shadowed by superstition and prejudices. But the honor, dignity, and virtue of man cannot be regarded as a prejudice. Similarly, every defense of peace will be neither a sign of fear nor of superstition. In every manifestation of this noble striving, there will already be expressed that love toward peace, which is ordained in all fundamental laws and creeds. "Blessed are the peacemakers."

Certainly, every insult of peace, every violation of a peaceful life, already contradicts positive human constructiveness. If a man is, as Plato says, *zoon politicon* (a social being), then in such a social structure, mankind should be first of all imbued with a veneration for peaceful relationships. This is not impotent pacificism but a virile and conscious defense of dignity, be this around the hearth or in a clan or in the state. How could the idea of the defense of dignity be non-peaceful? One can visualize a peaceful guard or a vigil in the name of peace, but essentially, in the heart of such a vigil, there should live the ideal of peace. This beneficial peace will not be like an ill-wishing neighbor; on the contrary, it will be a good neighbor, who honestly knows his borderline.

Conquest and annexation should be considered medieval. One may convince a man in the name of honor, reason, or the heart, but every act of violence will forever remain on the dark pages of the history of mankind.

Such persuasion, in the name of honor and dignity, is possible when a man is truly like Plato's "social being," and not a ferocious beast. But to be such a "social being," one has to exercise patience and tolerance to the highest extent. No one requires self-humiliation; it is ordained since ancient times that "self-humiliation is worse than pride." Of course, neither in superstition nor in hypocrisy and bigotry can any concept of peace and honor be established. If someone heralds peace while at the same time sharpening the dagger in his heart, this will not be peace but evil hypocrisy.

In the ancient Kainourgion of Byzantium, the majestic image of the Nikopoia was surrounded by inscriptions of prayers of parents for their children and of children for their parents. Thus, the most sacred and heartiest were exhibited in cold, official halls. From the history of Byzantium, we know that such inscriptions remained as dead conventionalities. In their formality they could not inspire or convince anyone; the complete downfall of the Byzantine Empire only proves that the dead word has nothing in common with life.

Innumerable hypocritical inscriptions left their shadows on the face of the earth. Precisely, these signs of hypocrisy turned many people away from the true understanding of the great, sacred foundations such as peace, honor, and dignity. He who knows how to affirm honor would have the right to speak of real peace. Without honor and honesty, what peace is altogether possible?

The fine for the violation of a peaceful state of life is an extremely precise and universal demand. It includes not only a violation of public safety, as foreseen by police regulations, but can cover a much wider and more necessary field. When we speak of the protection of cultural treasures, this will also be a struggle against the violation of a peaceful condition of life. When someone puts a lawful restraint against cruelty, this also will be a care for the same peaceful life. When people work for the elimination of everything harmful in human evolution, this also will be the defense of the same sacred and beautiful peace, the striving for which still exists in the depth of the hearts of mankind.

Innumerable sayings about peace exist in the covenants and laws of the East and the West. From the most ancient antiquity, there stand before our eyes the radiant images of great lawgivers—born peacemakers. In the whole classical world, one can trace many strivings to the same noble ideal. Not without reason have we now remembered the *fredum* of the old laws of the Franks. The period preceding the medieval ages was always considered the darkest epoch. But even from this epoch, despite the "price of blood," resounded the striving for the defense of peace.

"Peace unto the whole world!" For the realization of such a broad and sacred concept, one must abide by many peaceful conditions, the violation of which, even from the point of view of primitive laws, would be considered a crime. Let us not be misled by the idea that such peaceful understanding is regulated only by pompous international conferences. They exist in all of our relationships. Therefore, first of all, let us be extremely cordial and thoughtful toward each other. Let us realize the necessity of tolerance and patience. If we were to reiterate these foundations an endless number of times, it would not be superfluous according to the present conditions in the world. From obeisance to peaceful laws, there is born a renaissance of honor and dignity. These eternal concepts can never be considered as fossilized remnants but will remain forever as the basis of a wise and enlightened evolution.

The true safeguarding of peaceful conditions will attract to itself the success of which so much is said and for which so little is done. Nothing is easier than to break a precious vessel. But even if it be glued together, it will yet remain forever a damaged invalid. Therefore, create in benevolent inexhaustibility beautiful vessels. Adorn them by the best thoughts and dedicate these vessels of life in your innermost heart to the great peace of the world.

MUTATIS MUTANDIS

HISTORY gives us numerous examples, during ancient periods, of the results of gambling and games of chance. Even the most significant pages of history are filled with stories of how rulers became slaves, having lost by their gambling not only their wives and children but also their entire empires. Many poetic and dramatic works are based upon these demoralizing temptations. Even the great battle upon that most glorious field of Kurukshetra was caused by a loss in a game of dice.

It would seem as if the conditions of life have long since changed. New codes were laid into the foundation, presupposing a number of acts and consequences. Nevertheless, the press brought the strange information that because of the races and the enormous bets made upon them, the birthday celebration of the king had been postponed for another day. If one historian has become convinced, amazingly so, at the gigantic extent and consequences of a game of dice, then another historian, at some other period, might regard with amazement and condemnation such an obvious preference for speculation and games in place of a tribute to the head of an empire. The same history notes down the ancient benediction of arms before a mortal battle in the name of the very same God. Only recently we witnessed how numerous countries invoked the one and the same God to aid them in annihilating their enemies. Time was when we encountered the fact that the heads of empires took along with them their cooks in order to escape poisoning, and had a special person for the tasting of the food. Do not outstanding statesmen now have to employ the very same means?

One may endlessly bring similar comparisons. They will arouse the same exclamations of astonishment. But it is the same whether it occurred in hoary antiquity or whether it happens today in a somewhat changed aspect and attire. It means we have not advanced any further. Perhaps in antiquity, it even happened more frankly and more picturesquely, thus redeeming to a certain extent the inner hypocrisy and villainy. Besides, in ancient times there was less of the hypocritically written, and the laws of Manu, Hammurabi, and those of the first lawmakers were much briefer, although in many cases their conciseness made them far more impressive.

Since those ancient times, many new empires were born and passed into oblivion. There have been so many changes of rulers that the record of history could hardly encompass all these names; and only the testimonies of artists through a coin, a medal, or a stella bring us records of the new name, and a hint of one more conqueror who disappeared is given. But these changes cannot seem amazing when we are faced now with the colossal changes of the entire surface of the planet. When in addition to the half-legendary but already recognized Atlantis, we have an entire group of historic islands that have disappeared comparatively recently.

Some islands disappear, and other shores and peaks emerge. The soil, which seems to us so immovable and steadfast, is moving relatively only a little slower than the ocean waves. It would seem as though humanity ought to be accustomed, during its long life, to motion. And exactly this principle of relativity and motion ought, at last, to attract the attention of humanity on its own evolution. It was already the enlightened Marcus Aurelius who wrote the wise covenant, "Study the motion of the luminaries as one who participates in it." But this wise advice has thus far remained entirely without application. If humanity could rise in thoughts to the far-off worlds, then what a speedy and brilliant evolution would be consummated.

I know that you will speak about all the newest discoveries, calling them "the crown of evolution." You speak about isolated brilliant theories, which are read in leisure time. Finally, you speak about the customs of so-called civilized life, which now permit to the broad masses what some time ago was only possessed by rulers and supreme priests. It is true that our cities, while poisoning the human organism and creating a crippled generation, already give provide some possibilities for utilizing the new discoveries. But we do not speak about the sewerage systems of civilization. We do not speak of canned vegetables nor yet about canned music. We speak of that which gives impulse to the best aspiration of humanity.

Only recently we have lived through a terrific war. We are aware that, in this decade, the consequences of war have not only been erased but, on the contrary, have crystallized and swelled into a real misery. They have become a misery well-nigh irreparable, which can only be altered in essence by unsuspected measures. How often at our school or university desk have we heard the old advice "*Mutatis mutandis*"? "Change that which ought to be changed." Since then, a multitude of barbaric facts of war and peacetimes have invaded life. Humanity may once more be convinced of how at the very time when those most sincere were perishing upon the battlefields as victims of world calamities, the wide adaptations were treacherously fattening themselves upon the blood of others. What diabolic inventiveness was expressed by the dark ones in order to find a thousand ways for personal gain, in full knowledge of how destructively this looting would react upon the growing generations. And now, if a secret ballot were taken as to who is for war and who is against it, it is impossible to know what the results of this secret ballot would be. Of course, a multitude of women would vote against war, and cultured circles, as well as many of the working masses, would no doubt revolt against the misery. But let us not believe that the number of black ballots would be small. What a variety of ramifications the roots of meanness possess, and what sad and unique reasons will be given in order to go back again to the irresponsible time when everything was permitted and everything could be explained by hypocritical participation in a common work! It is fearful to remember the criminal negotiations for rotten and sometimes even non-existing material. It is horrifying for human dignity to look back at the fraudulent documents, criminal recriminations, and commands that were the cause of peril to many thousands of people.

"But this has passed," you will say. Since then, we have already had such a multitude of facts, conferences, and financial agreements. Such and such plan has been fulfilled, but as a result we have increased depression. Old-fashioned ships have been disarmed and even destroyed in order that they should be replaced by still more harmful constructions. Even in shops, we have taken care to see that the air should be ozonized, while at the same time, the scientific laboratories have utilized their facilities in inventing new poisonous gases. Does not the scientist in the field of chemistry who has invented the most deadly gas dream of receiving the prize for chemistry from the same committee that gives the peace award? Even now, some people dream of such an achievement of science as would, with one fratricidal dispatch, kill entire populated regions. And perhaps, another enlightened scientist dreams about the "successful" poisoning of all waters, in order that everything alive should perish. To this, someone may answer that it is not the scientists who are inventing such murderous forces but that it is the technicians, the engineers. No, dear readers, without scientific knowledge such murderous brutality could not be invented. And was it not a scientist who discovered the death ray and who, by the very command of special justice, departed to the infernal regions together with his venomous inventions?

But things could be simpler if the scientists could give an oath, similar to that of physicians, not to permit out of their laboratories any injurious discoveries. The more so because many of these terrible gases and rays could, perhaps with the addition of one ingredient, be turned into a true benefit of humanity.

Mutatis mutandis. In the days of profoundest calamities, one must speedily change that which ought to be changed. And first of all, one ought to change that which is harmful into that which is beneficial. Do not play the roles of fools, as if you did not know what was of benefit. Every human heart knows in its depth perfectly well where is the common benefit, the benefit for the nearest one and, at the same time, benefit for oneself. For nowhere in creativeness is self-destruction demanded. The true common benefit is also a benefit for oneself because one is a part of the community. Let me emphasize, it is also the benefit for oneself because one is part of the community.

By changing that which is harmful into the beneficial, namely, replacing criminal destruction by construction, we will do that which is needed for evolution. We will do that which is needed not only for the evolution of civilization, but for evolution-culture. Someone in a spell of madness has tried to conceive of a corporation that would undertake the erection of a shaft that would reach the most incalculable depths and would be filled with the newest, most terrific explosives, which would split the planet by an unprecedented explosion. The plan is a mad one. But in its very rashness, it deserves more attention than the inventions of new deadly gases. And the secret countenancing of narcotics, which were glorious in their past, deteriorates entire generations and kills entire nations. Must not this scourge of humanity, which is more perilous than syphilis, cancer, and tuberculosis, be exterminated from life? And cannot each one of us name a multitude of problems that deserve immediate extermination from life?

The best ones, the enlightened ones, must undeferrably unite for opposition against darkness, ignorance, distortion, and treason. These best ones must unite in all countries, not for the sake of police measures and counteractions, which demand forbiddances, but in the name of light and education as such. Feeling in one's heart the undeferrability of the evolution of culture, this luminous League of Culture, casting aside all petty conventionalities, must unite and, for the bliss of humanity, must actively change that which must be changed.

Mutatis mutandis!

ROOTS OF CULTURE

OLD recollections: Many years have passed since we laid the foundation of the Master Institute of United Arts. How unnoticeably these years have gone by! This is because during a multitude of circumstances and events, time moves with especial rapidity. As if it were yesterday, one recalls how, with M. M. Lichtmann, we were hurrying to rent a space in the Hotel des Artistes in New York. By accident, we found ourselves delayed on the way; and due to this delay, as we entered the subway, we were accosted by a Greek artist with the most unexpected, extraordinary exclamation—

"I have been looking for you for three months already! Do you need a large studio?". . . "Of course, we do. Where is it?". . . "In the building of the Greek church on 54th Street.". . . "All right, tomorrow we will go look at it.". . . "No, impossible! I cannot keep it any longer. If you wish to see it, let us go at once!"

And so, instead of the Hotel des Artistes, we are seated with Father Lazaris of the Greek Cathedral who insists that I must be of the clergy. And, here, we decide to rent the space. And under the Cross of the Greek Cathedral is laid the foundation of the long-since conceived Institute of United Arts. It is a large studio, but only one room.

Someone says to us, "Could you possibly dream of having an Institute of United Arts in one studio?". . . I answer, "For the conception of creation, one does not need a room larger than the cell of Fra Angelico. Each tree must grow. If the work is vital, it will develop. If it is destined to die, in any case it will have to die in one room." And so the first piano studies resound through the studio, and the first dreams about painting, and vocal and sculpture classes are realized. Soon the studio has to be divided into three parts, and life itself supports the idea of unity.

Those connected with us are such experienced, creative guides—Giles, Serge, Mordkin, the Lichtmanns, Grant, Germanova, Bisttram, Andoga, Wagenar, and Appia. Already we have seventy coworkers, working in different departments, and hundreds of students fill the classes and halls. Already the new generation of teachers is growing, and Ellen Kettunen, Frieda Lazaris, Linda Cappabianca, and others of our pupils form the second line of attack. Twelve years ago, based on long academic experience, I decisively affirmed the following statement:

"Art will unify Humanity. Art is one—indivisible. Art has its many branches, yet all are one. Art is the manifestation of the coming synthesis. Art is for all. Everyone will enjoy true art. The Gates of the 'Sacred Source' must be wide open for everybody, and the light of art will influence numerous hearts with a new love. At first this feeling will not be perceived, but, after all, it will purify the human consciousness, and how many young hearts are searching for something real and beautiful! So give it to them. Bring art to the people where it belongs. We should have not only museums, theatres, universities, public libraries, railway stations, and hospitals, but even prisons that are decorated and beautified. Then we will have no more prisons."

I remember, at that time, that certain friends smiled to each other and whispered, "Beautiful dreams, but how will life react to them?" Because our chief principle is "Admittance and benevolence." We and our coworkers do not like the dead "No," and with each possibility make the effort to say, "Yes." It is not without reason that all people express their affirmation by an open sound and for negation have chosen the dumb, semi-bestial "No."

What other considerations have been confirmed by the experience of the last ten years? Life has confirmed that all unity is useful, has confirmed that it is practical (we do not fear this word) to have various branches of art under one roof—having one common library, a common office, a common artistic activity, and the closest intercourse between the separate branches. It is practical to afford the students the opportunity of trying their forces in various branches until they finally make their choice. It is practical that there be an interchange of thought among musicians, artists, and designers. It is practical to show full trust in the teacher, letting him manifest his methods in life. The results will indicate whether he is right because, as is with one's entire life, we must judge by the result. It is practical to give possibilities to students to try their forces in life as soon as possible, teaching them courage and safeguarding them from vulgarity. It is practical, as was carried out by Howard Giles and Emil Bisttram, to have music during the work in art classes and to give lectures that, by their artistic and philosophic content, may raise and unite the spirit of the entire artistic working guild.

It is practical to give examples from the history of art; thus, we will once more learn to what extent art was the creative, peaceful basis for the entire life of the state. Chiefly, one must reject less, remembering that the majority of denials have ignorance as their basis; thus, teachers turn into guides, transmitting to students not only technique but also life experience, sharing with them the valuable acquisitions that will prove a strong shield for the new generation.

How often humanity, entangled in its problems, attempted to deny the significance of the teacher. In epochs of decadence, it was seemingly possible to shake the basic conception of the Spiritual Hierarchy. But not for long did this darkness last. With the epochs of renaissance, again the great leadership of teaching was inevitably crystallized, and people again began to feel the ladder of ascent and the blessed hand of the Leader. Many times small minds hesitate, fearing that they may be oppressed by the personality of the Teacher. Especially those who have little to lose worry most often lest they lose something. In this regard, we now enter a very significant epoch. In certain strata of humanity, the spirit of denial has just succeeded in evoking a protest against the Teacher. But as always happens, denial can arise only temporarily, and the creative origins of humanity will again lead the wanderers of life into the path of affirmation, of fearless search—to the path of creation and beauty. People again remember about the Teachers. Of course, these Teachers must not pertain to a grandfather's study with all its petrified remains.

The Teacher is He who reveals, enlightens, and encourages: He who will say, "Blessed are the obstacles, through them we grow." He who will recall the beautiful Golgothas of knowledge and art because therein lies creative achievement. He who is able to remind, to teach the means of achievement will not be rejected by strong spirits. He Himself will realize the value of the Hierarchy of Knowledge, and in his constant movement will create the ascending researches.

So many schools and useful disseminators of knowledge can be organized. To all of them, the same advice can be given: Each tree can be planted only as a small sapling. Only gradually will it become tried and find steady roots. Therefore, if there is a hardened desire to help the dissemination of knowledge and beauty, let it be fulfilled without delay. Let it not be handicapped by small possibilities. Practically, it is not in the size but in the inner substance of the seed.

VI
LET US HOPE

PEACE TO ALL BEINGS

"Whoever thinks evil of it in his heart,
Let his heart rot!
Whoever stretches his hand toward it,
Let his hand be cut off!
Whoever harms it with his eye,
May his eye become blind!
Whoever does any harm to this bridge
May that creature be born in hell!"

THESE lines, about the first bridge across the Indus, were written by Naglug, the Buddhist ruler of Ladakh, who ever tried to instill in the population a respect for all that is constructive. The good king Asoka also gave first place to construction, and the Blessed One Himself never tired of sounding the call to constructive effort.

A short time before He passed away, He exclaimed: "How beautiful is Vaisali."

Such holy teachings were spread abroad by Buddhist preachers, and no one can point to destruction on the part of a Buddhist.

Enlightenment and construction are the panacea that is at the basis of all Buddhist teachings.

Is it the moment to talk of peace when wars are raging? Certainly it is now that we ought to proclaim, on all hands, the doctrine of peace, enlightenment, and goodwill.

Peace cannot be imposed by governmental decrees. True peace will only be secured when the nations realize the vanity of quarreling and mutual destruction.

Peace that results in dishonor and enslavement can never bring happiness.

Only peace that arises from tireless efforts to construction and enlightenment can bring happiness.

Some people think that as long as the cannon is not roaring, peace can be maintained. It is the roar of the heart, however, and not the noise of the cannon that provokes war.

Many never tire of repeating, "What is the use of preaching peace in these days when, as in the case of China, we see hecatombs of cruelty and bloodshed? Such calls to peace are only hollow phrases, abstract ideals."

One could answer that murderers and destroyers have always existed on our long-suffering earth, and alas! They will last for a long time yet, but, let us hope, not forever.

Meanwhile, the penal laws and commandments are not only being decreed but applied to life. And so it is with peace. Even if we allow that this blessed word "peace" is for many a mere abstraction, nevertheless we know that the order "Peace to all beings" has been proclaimed. And the order is not merely an abstract idea but something that we have to apply.

He who gave such an order knew very well the true path for humanity.

Only active enlightenment can give us a proper perception of the world.

"Peace through Culture"—we will never tire of repeating this truth. If it has not yet become a truism, this is because the consciousness of all nations has not been saturated with this sole way of reaching the highest good.

To understand the real meaning of peace, one ought to be conscious of the real treasures of humanity, for he who is conscious of such values and really understands them will know how to preserve them.

Museums and universities in which history and archaeology are taught are not enough because they only deal with the formal aspect of these subjects. What we have in mind is not the dead letter and the formal side of these studies but rather the awakening of consciousness in the hearts of the nations.

Many times we have had occasion, with our own eyes, to see these senseless ruins that are the shameful monuments of human ignorance. We have seen the most beautiful monuments ruined, the finest sculptures shattered or destroyed, and all through the criminal ignorance of their value.

Such vestiges of destructive mania ought to warn us to be careful with these irreplaceable treasures.

We have recently heard of a plan to bury all artistic monuments under sandbags. Quite apart from the practical inconvenience of such a project, we should realize that sandbags alone will never suffice, and that only culture is powerful enough to protect the beautiful. Thus, we should hasten to repeat on all hands "Peace through Culture."

Why do I speak of the protection of art treasures on this memorable day? It is not merely to avail myself of such an occasion. I have other reasons. On memorable days people recall the highest principles. When, therefore, all of our friends are ready to repeat the commandment "Peace to all Beings," let them think of the way that leads to peace. Let them remember how carefully all cultural treasures ought to be preserved because this alone can lead toward the future gateway of peace.

"Peace to all Beings."

This sign of the triad, which is to be found all over the world, may have several meanings. Some interpret it as a symbol of the past, present, and future enclosed in the ring of eternity. Others consider that it refers to religion, science, and art held together in the circle of culture. But whatever the interpretation, the sign itself is of the most universal character.

The oldest of Indian symbols *Chintamani*, the sign of happiness is composed of this symbol, and one can find it in the Temple of Heaven in Peking. It appears in the Three Treasures of Tibet, on the breast of the Christ in Memling's well-known painting, on the Madonna of

Strasbourg; on the shields of the Crusaders, and the coat of arms of the Templars. It can be seen on the blades of the famous Caucasian swords known as Gurda.

It appears as a symbol in a number of philosophical systems; it can be found on the images of Gessar Khan and Rigden Djapo; on the "Tamga" of Timurlane, and on the coat of arms of the Popes. It is to be seen in the works of ancient Spanish painters and of Titian, and on the ancient ikons of St. Nicholas in Bari and that of St. Sergius and the Holy Trinity.

It can be found on the coat of arms of the city of Samarkand, on Ethiopian and Coptic antiquities, on the rocks of Mongolia, on Tibetan rings, on the breast ornaments of Lahul, Ladakh, and all the Himalayan countries, and on the pottery of the Neolithic Age.

It is conspicuous on Buddhist banners. The same sign is branded on Mongolian steeds. Nothing, then, could be more appropriate for assembling all the races than this symbol, which is no mere ornament but a sign that carries with it a deep meaning.

It has existed for immense periods of time and is to be found throughout the world. No one, therefore, can pretend that it belongs to any particular sect, confession, or tradition, and it represents the evolution of consciousness in all its varied phases.

When it is a question of defending the world's treasures, no better symbol could be selected, for it is universal, of immense antiquity, and carries with it a meaning that should find an echo in every heart.

Today, when humanity is burying its treasures to save them from destruction, the Banner of Peace stands for other principles. It affirms that works of art and of genius are universal and above national distinctions; it proclaims, "*Noli me tangere.*" "Do not treat the world's treasures in a sacrilegious way."

Peace to all beings!

MIR

MIR—this word in Russian means both the Universe and peace. Not without reason are these two great conceptions united in one sound. If one imagines the Universe one also realizes peaceful labor. Beginning work, one also becomes conscious of the Universe.

People talk about peace especially when they are afraid of war. But there are different kinds of war: internal and external, visible and invisible. Which of them are more horrible remains to be seen. . . .

Indeed, the worst calamity for ancient and present humanity is that their greatest poet, the wise, blind Homer, appeared to be a bard of war and not of peace. Together with his faith in the gods, he also lost faith in peace:

> There is and there can be no union
> > between lions and men.
> Wolves and sheep cannot live in
> > hearty concord.
> Eternal foes they are—hostile against
> > each other.
> Hence, between us, love is impossible.
> > No concordats
> Can exist between us until one is
> > slain,
> Feeding with his blood the fierce
> > god Ares. *

---

* The *Iliad*, Book XXII.

This means that "everyone will kill each other." "In the Universe there will be no end of war. . . ."

Through the *Iliad*—the war of Troy— begins endless war, which throughout ages lasts until our days!" exclaims Merezhkovsky. There are many soul-stirring lamentations. And Dante has round, infernally burning abodes for murderers and all malefactors.

And there are also other testimonies.

On the Eastern shore of Crete in Palaikastro—the ancient Heleia, which was the capital of the island about 1400 BC—there was found an ancient hymn, one of the most beautiful and simple prayers of humanity:

> Great Cronus, rejoice,
> O Ruler of joy—rejoice!
> Thou proceedest
> Leading the spirit.
> Come to us on the mount of Dictea
> And rejoice in song and dance!
> Let us greet Thee on lutes
> With flute accompaniment,
> And let us sing encircling
> The infallible Altar.
> For here, Thou,
> The Immortal Child,
> Was hidden by shield-bearing guardians
> Who accepted Thee from Rhea.
> And many fruitful years commenced
> And mortals cognized the truth,
> And even wild beasts were tamed
> By all-blissful Peace!

Mir—peace; in this one word is expressed the whole essence. "To live in peace means never to raise arms against each other." This commandment was given in all languages, in all ages.

And on the Eastern side is Cronus, and on the Western side, Quetzalcoatl—both are messengers of peace; they both "close their ears when they hear of war." In Canaan, Melchizedek, the king of Salem—the King of Peace—blesses Abraham in the name of Adonai, the God of Peace. Thus, in all religions, the first word is "peace."

When one studies symbols and tablets, one will find in all images and hieroglyphics the same desire—the sacred prayer for peace.

"Do not do evil to animals" is the ordainment of Triptolemus, the messenger sent by Demeter to savage people after the great flood; Triptolemus was to teach people agriculture and to uplift them from the bestial to human life. "Do not do evil to animals" in Biblical language means: "Blessed be those who have pity for everything living" because "all living beings suffer together and wail up till now." They suffer together with man, they perish with man, or they are saved with him.

Should man kill animals in order to feed on meat? No, by no means, ordains Demeter, the fruit-bearing goddess. With bloody food there enters into man the spirit of killing, the spirit of war, but the spirit of peace enters only through bloodless food.

And Hesiod, the shepherd on Mount Helicon sings:

> "God made it a law for beasts, birds,
>   and fishes
> To devour each other—because they do not
>   know the Truth.
> But to man, God gave the Truth!"

The truth does not kill! For everyone, it is always possible not to kill, not to make war. If you kill, you will die; give life, and you will live. A child understands this, and yet this is the mystery of mysteries!

Should one defend culture? Yes, one should, always and in everything.

Should one help the workers of culture, the depressed and burdened? Yes, one should, always and in everything.

Should one unite around the sign of culture in order

to conquer the attempts of destruction and decay? Yes, one should, always and in everything.

Perhaps culture, knowledge, and beauty are sufficiently guarded and affirmed? No, they are not.

Perhaps everywhere the foundations of culture are already strongly fortified? No, unfortunately, they are not.

Perhaps the workers for culture are especially safeguarded by law and in the consciousness of the people? We wish it were so!

And the League of Culture, as the voice of public opinion, is indeferrably needed!

We have to invoke peace—non-killing. What does this mean! Is it possible that millenniums have not taught people that which has been ordained by all Commandments? But what do we see? The further we go, the more one has to reiterate the necessity of peace. Where is evolution when a monster gun is already loaded and death-bringing poison is madly sown? People have became so skillful that poison and death already fall from the blue sky—from the same blessed sky from whence was bestowed only blissful prana, the panacea.

What has happened? Under the ground there are explosive mines and threatening gangways! From the blue sky comes poison and death! The barrels of gigantic guns are proudly raised. Soon there will probably be a "festival of the shell," when it accomplishes a flight around the world, when it will destroy everything that can be destroyed.

"People cannot guess beforehand in what terrible danger humanity stands in case of a new war"— Prof. Andre Meier. "The poison gases of the last war are child's play in comparison with what we will see if a new war breaks out," adds another expert, Prof. Cannon of Columbia University. According to Dr. Hilton Jones of New York, a newly invented gas can destroy a whole army as easily as "blowing out a candle."

Truth! The inventor of poison believes that he creates truth. The makers of guns are proud that their tools will annihilate a man even beyond the horizon. The forger of the sword anticipates that his steel will penetrate all hearts. . . . Such are the thoughts of man!

Helas, not such a truth is needed! "Mankind needs another truth," says Gorky: a truth that will blissfully, strengthen creative energy." A truth is needed that will stimulate mutual trust and striving toward goodwill.

Others make impenetrable armor and shields. Perhaps they hope to create a defense against all evil influx? Let it be so.

The defense of culture, the defense of the motherland, the defense of human dignity does not think of violent usurpation. . . . The armor of defense is not the poison of destruction. Defense is justified and attacks are condemned.

It has some special meaning that, in Russian, *mir* is synonymous for peace and for the Universe. This synonym is not due to a poverty of the language. Indeed, the language is rich. They are synonymous in their essence. Verily, the Universe and a peaceful creativeness are indivisible. From ancient times this salutary synonym had a special mission.

Mir—the Universe and *mir*—the peaceful, universal labor; a creative sowing, the beauty of the world—the conqueress.

SEALS

MUCH is said about the ancient Chinese seals that have been found in Ireland. The antiquity of these seals refers to several centuries before our era, some even think several thousands of years. On the basis of these seals, the question is debated as to the ancient relationships of Ireland with China. Others observe that there could have been an intermediary point in Egypt or Crete, which had a long-standing relationship with both the Far East and with the British Isles, the latter of which served as the source of certain metals.

Indeed, all such questions require many confirmations and complementary facts, but, nevertheless, the discovery of ancient Chinese seals in Ireland reminds us again about the extension of long-distance relationships in the remotest times. Long ago, we had occasion to find amber in kurgans from the Stone Age, in Koenigsberg, Central Russia. In Neolithic times, before the knowledge of metals, relationships were demonstrated at quite extensive distances.

All archaeological findings, the uniformity of many discovered types, and finally, the details of ornament, rituals, and the other elements of their way of life indicate not only a community of the feelings common to man but also unquestionable relationships at long distances. The similarity of the alphabet not long ago discovered in Harappa and Mohenjo-daro, India, with depictions on Easter Island, also indicates noteworthy international relationships many centuries before our era.

Without any difficulty it is possible to discern how entire protracted periods confirm the development of international relationships; and then, as it were, there comes on a strange tribal forgetfulness, a timorous immobility, and the memory of former relationships is wiped away. In itself the memory of peoples represents an extraordinarily interesting manifestation. To contemporary man, it sometimes seems perfectly inadmissible that, in any manner, entire peoples could forget about something already fully known to them. The facts and allusions in ancient chronicles indicate the possibility of just such a strange forgetfulness.

Many of the completely lost technical methods of Egypt, the existence of gunpowder in ancient China, the details of various lost techniques of Babylon, certain objects of the Mayan culture—all this reminds one about the fact that very essential discoveries, incomprehensible to us, have been forgotten in their entirety. Moreover, such forgetfulness does not always coincide with epochs of advancement or decline. It is precisely as if some other psychological or even physiological facts have altered the channel of the current of popular thought.

Amid all the misunderstandings and presuppositions, the question of the most ancient international relationships always proves very complicated, yet it is especially interesting from the point of view of peace. The discovery of objects of definite antiquity in remote countries is a material sign of some relationships, the more so when the objects are found in ethnographical strata, which actually belong to former cultures of life. Something extremely inspiring is contained in these substantial signs, which are actually embodied in these seals of national relationships.

And again at present, in certain countries inertness and immobility are so clearly manifested, in that there are inhabitants of certain cities who are proud of that fact that they have never had to go beyond the limits of their native city, or that they even succeeded in keeping themselves from crossing a river that flows through the city. There are all sorts of droll people. But among the strangest extravagances, such a prejudice of immobility always remains one of the most striking. Yet what a great number of people exist who have never glanced beyond the limits of their country! Only in recent years has travel re-entered, as it were, a program of self-education. Whereas from remote antiquity, voices have been borne to us calling out about the usefulness of travel and of international knowledge.

The celebrated, everlastingly mentioned Marco Polo must be looked upon as a collective name. Frequently by this name are meant the infinite number of travelers who have been the bearers of international relationships. The name of Marco Polo has become firmly fixed in history, but indeed a great number of names, of ancient beaten paths, remain unknown. But that is not the question. Of course, any historical name becomes not so much a name as a concept. It is precisely this, that on ancient discovered objects, we see marks incomprehensible to us, which now serve us as conventional signs, yet which formerly were the personal seals of some firms or of some definite individuals.

Each reminder about international relationships is, as it were, a new seal upon the human peace treaty. Not so long ago in London, a certain Spaniard, Madariaga, delivered quite a pompous speech about the price of peace. No bombasting abstractions are the substantial signs of peace, but, first of all, the material seals of world relationships.

People are actually thinking about peace—some self-interestedly, others selflessly. In all cases there is required some sign, the substantial seal of the fact that outside of human violence and hatred, there have been possible peaceful relationships in the different domains of business.

The price of peace is defined as living human merit and dignity, as benevolence of heart, broadly embracing and noble. Not by denials of cultural treasures but by recognition of the creativeness of good is the price of peace defined and established.

Archaeology as a science based on material memorials is manifested right now as an assistant in many scientific and social considerations. And, likewise, in the question of the price of peace, archaeology can bring many of the most precious signs. From long-forgotten ruins, from abandoned burial places and the remains of palaces and cities can be adduced material proofs of peaceful international relationships. In semi-historical writings in old hieroglyphics, the story reaches one's ears about how, in fragile boats and on wearied horses, man penetrated remote regions, not only in warlike fury but also with a good desire for peaceful exchange. Underneath these narratives will be placed, as it were, material seals, ratifying the human peace treaties.

In the creativeness of good, it is always possible to come to terms, for only in a paroxysm of malice or of dark misanthropy are peaceful advancements impossible! Long ago it was said in various tongues, "He who lifts up the sword will also perish by the sword," and he will perish in a preordained hour that will perhaps be for him quite unexpected. And so it is in each quarrel and in each dissension.

The seals did not ratify quarrelsome contracts. The seals were affixed to a document of some relationships, of some business establishments. Yet in each true business will be the element of peace. A victory through beneficial signs will be a most radiant and striking victory. It is possible to kill with a serpent sting but not conquer, for to conquer will mean to convince. In such prices of peace, let us refer carefully to all material signs. It would have seemed inordinate to connect Easter Island with Harappa, India, or, now, Ireland with China. Yet what is impossible at present? Seals or depicted hieroglyphs are fully convincing. "Peace on earth, goodwill to man" is also imperative, for goodwill is engendered in the heart. And what is more substantial than the human heart in all of its inspired ascent?

Man should rejoice at each seal of peaceful relationships. Each sign of remote international agreements is a pledge of the possibility of future treaties, heartfelt and unbreakable. At one time, savage warriors devoured the hearts of the vanquished, but now in each peaceful relationship, let people remember about the living heart. The seals of antiquity are for the future.

DAY OF GLORY

VADE, filii, ad Montes Indiae et ad cavernas suas, et accipe ex cis lapides honoratos! "Go, my son, to the Mountains of India, and to their quarries, and take from there those precious stones!"

So speaks the most excellent Hali, the Arabian, mentioned by Paracelsus. Let us go to the Mountains of India!

"*Sophia cum Moria Certamen*," published in *Summum Bonum*, also discusses the Mountain and the glorious treasures therein contained. And again, Paracelsus justly assures us: "*Nihil est opertus quod non revelábitur.*" "There is nothing so hidden, that it will not be revealed!"

"Lumen de Lumine" outlines the conditions of the path to the mysterious Mountain: "Only follow your Guide, who will offer Himself to you and will meet you on the way. This Guide will bring you to the Mountain. You need neither sword nor any other bodily weapons. Be resolute and take heed that you return not, for your Guide will not suffer any evil to befall you."

And from another part of the world, the voice of Athanasius Nikitin Tveritin, a Muscovite of the fifteenth century, reaches us. After his journey to India, he exclaimed, "And I, out of the midst of many troubles, went to India!"

Love India!

The Mountains of India, the Resplendent Himavat, are imbued with powerful energies for the strengthening of body and spirit. Here were raised numerous glorious *viharas*, the ruins of which still adorn the mountain ranges. Only to think, that in these places the Blessed

One had Himself imprinted His footsteps. Here is the road to the Holy Kailash; here are the paths to the Sacred Manasarovar Lake; here are the caves of Milarepa and Lake Ravalsar—the abode of Padma Sambhava. Up to now, hosts of pilgrims search for the hidden sacred books, which are concealed in the ancient country of Zahor, which today is known as Mandi. In memorable places in Kuluta, the hill people still point at ruins, stating that here were ancient *stupas*, under the foundation of which books are concealed. We have ourselves seen these places and were told that the hidden books cannot be revealed until the predestined date.

And in hill temples you can find, besides other statues, the Image of the Blessed Tathagata and of Avalokiteśvara. There are the paths to the Holy Triloknath, where both Buddhists and Sadhus meet and along the way one find on the rocks gigantic carvings of the Blessed One and Maitreya. Thus, even in those places where ancient *viharas* are in ruins, there live solid traditions of the Great Message.

There are different opinions as to whether to celebrate memorable days. Some consider them as matters of the past and pass them without attention, but for others, such festive days are beneficial milestones on the path toward the future. Ask true seekers and friends whether they wish to neglect such days, which have forever been for them guardians and messengers—and they will not want to reject these days of joy.

Is it not wonderful that Vesak Day will be celebrated all over the world!

More than once, we had occasion to remind of the healing effects of union in spirit. People understand with difficulty that thought creates precisely. One constantly meets with surprise when asserting that thought is more creative than word and action. But during the uniting at memorable days, it is fit to remember how beneficially works thought that is simultaneously directed to the Common Good. During the great days, when we gather in cooperation and goodwill, there should especially be expressed the thought of real friendship and untiring striving. This will not be a selfish thought, for it will resound not about the self but for general construction. And there will be no doubt in such thought because it will be adamant in its exaltation toward Bliss. During such a solemn hour, there will be no irritation or anger because all know the harm of self-poisoning. But there will be, during the hour, a special solemnity not marred by the dusty routine of every day. The realization of Great Service will strengthen the vigor of the spirit and will be the best quality of the Golden Path.

Everyone dreams of friends, whether known or unknown. And during festive days, thoughts especially reverberate at the same time in various parts of the world; similarly, good wishes are being sent into space, which are the foundations of real friendship. Verily, this day will be greeted with flowers and special meetings and cordial discussions. And if anyone happens to be alone on this day, he will not feel lonely if he surrounds himself with images, radiant recollections, and inspiring strivings.

Memorable days in a spiritual, social, and family aspect affirm the solemnity of life. People beautify themselves both bodily and spiritually, and such a day, in every respect, becomes radiantly significant.

Among the best mental sendings, there will always be predominant the thought of peace unto the whole world. Among the best mental sendings, there will always predominate the thought of peace unto the whole world. Everywhere this prayer is being expressed. The peace of the world is being built up through great struggle and labor. And yet every human heart in its innermost will responds to this Command of Light.

Let us also remember, on this solemn day, about peace for the whole world. If in every dwelling there will radiate the sign of peace unto the whole world, then will this call resound all over the globe.

Peace to all beings.

NOBLE VICTORY

IN the rays of the blessed future glimmers the Great Peace. But real peace can abide only there, where true culture dwells.

Friends! Put aside all recollections of the past and reaffirm with the heroes: "Forward! Forward! Forward!" *War Armageddon is over; now humanity is facing an Armageddon of culture.*

From remote ages a noble struggle was noted as a foundation of life. There should be joy in such a perpetual struggle. What gives this joy? The idea of a plough-field and of sowing seed! Verily the seeds of future achievements are sown in an untiring struggle. Whether it is a crowded city or a fragrant desert, the same struggle takes place everywhere. We must learn to love this struggle. Is it easy though? But if one will succeed once, fighting for truth, for general welfare, one will not feel the burden of struggle. New strength will arise.

But it is necessary to repeat over and over again about the essential points of struggle. There will be the moments of plunging. Let us know about such hindrances. Let us not be surprised when we hear about the oppression of our friends. Such moments are unavoidable. We will not overload ourselves, but we will inhale the fresh *prana*. Let us think of something most precious. Let the tide run. The ebb and flow is the pulse. "This, too, will pass." New possibilities will burst out unexpectedly there, where reason does not even suspect them.

In everything new, there is the potential for a new struggle. And there is no way of avoiding it. The best encouragement for us will be to know that with us remain the desirable people, while against us are those who must be our enemies. It would be bad if the enemies of your very nature were to agree with your actions. Let them always attack and threaten and, thus, increase your strength.

The idea of struggle is not a truism. The diversity of life creates the boundaries of struggle. Observe the earthquake. Everything begins to move, to crack, to fail. Everything proves to be movable; one cannot tell where is the limit and where the boundary.

To struggle for truth means to create welfare. Every struggle against lies, hypocrisy, injustice, and ignorance is beautiful. Who knows where and how will ripen the fruits of a heroic struggle? And what kind of gardens will blossom from the seeds of goodness and labor? And whom will they nourish? But the fragrance will be salutary. And we cannot tell where it will be particularly necessary. It is hard sometimes, but otherwise there would be no struggle. And again, how joyful it is to know that the enemies are those who should be the ones! The violent struggle, the irremovable watchfulness! Long ago it was said, "If you are tired, start again. If you are exhausted, start over and over again."

SACRED UNITY

OPEN in all schools the path to creative effort, to the greatness of art. Develop the creative instinct from the earliest years of childhood. Open up the paths of blessing.

The arts are one. What is the creative spirit that inheres in all art but a breath from the finer ethers of "worlds before and after"? Music, painting, sculpture, poetry, drama, and dance—these are one in essence, one in principle. Do they not spring from the one source—the broadly creative spirit? Are they not all parts of the one life? As petals interwoven and blended, they form the flower of life. They have their home in the timeless and the endless. That is why a single life is only long enough to catch "hints of the proper craft, tricks of the tool's true play."

To be in harmony with the increasing rate of life's vibration, we find we must make use of the fast-flying wings of the imagination. In our effort to join the worlds within and the worlds without, to converge on our "one world," we are rediscovering this principle of unity as relating to all life. For the basis of true culture, it would seem, lies in the perception not only of the unity of the arts but of the unity between art and living. These cannot be dissociated without harm. Where they are severed, life is fragmentized and crippled. Seen as one, it becomes an inexhaustible fountain of beauty. When we function truly with the wisdom of joy, it is with the whole consciousness. In the life of wholeness, as exemplified in the Academy of United Arts, the spirit of each of the arts and of life itself is finely fused and integrated.

Through varying art symbols, the student sees a world

garmented in many veils of beauty—a world "where music and silence and dreaming are one." He learns to seek the goal in creative labor—in striving to become, in the words of Dante, the "Scribe of Eternal Love." Through this service, "he develops enlarged capacities of perception and containment. He finds that the home of the true artist is thus "bounded by the mother-skies"; that "his race is Man, his banner—the Banner of Peace."

When, then, we are concerned about preserving cultural values, such excursions through all parts of the state will be the living custodians of the tradition of culture. Where, instead of destruction born of despair, there is awakened a living home-building, there blooms also a garden of beauty.

What has been said is no abstraction. These affirmations have been tested by many experiences in different parts of the world. Everywhere the human heart remains a true heart and is fed by the beautiful nourishment of culture.

I recall a beautiful Persian story. Several artisans on a journey had to pass a very wearisome night in a wild locality. But each one had with him his tools, and in some ruins was found a fallen beam. And here, during the watch hours, each one of the craftsmen applied his own lofty art to dressing the piece of wood. A woodcarver executed the figure of a beautiful girl; a tailor fashioned a garment. Then she was adorned in every way, with the result that a spiritual person with them inspired life in the beautifully created image. As always, the tale ends in full happiness, at the basis of which lay craftsmanship in various domains.

Another story tells how one of the caliphs, being taken captive and wishing to convey news about the place of his imprisonment, wove a rug with conventional signs, as a result of which he was liberated. But for this means of rescue, the caliph had to be a skillful weaver.

Yet again, I recollect a wise covenant of Gameliel: "Not

having educated his son in arts and crafts, he prepared him for brigandage on the highway." We need not recall the multitude of other highly poetic and practical covenants, but we urgently direct the attention of the Institute to such possibilities of highly useful, outside work.

Freedom! Freedom! Art as the highest expression of human consciousness must be free to lead humanity.

"Beauty will save the world."

Freedom! Freedom! Art is the beloved child of freedom. All superficial ephemerids could not stop the victorious path of art, of pure human joy. After all, to what "school" belonged Leonardo da Vinci, Michelangelo, Raphael, El Greco, Rembrandt, and other heroes of art? They created their own style, their own glorious path.

We who are witnessing the Armageddon of culture, we affirm that even the Machine Age with all of its "machine-minded" followers, even the tyrannical technocracy, will never suppress the freedom of creativeness.

Satyam, shivam, sundaram.

9 781947 016446